T✡E
WRONG JEW

DEFEATING THOSE
WHO WANT US DEAD

HESH KESTIN

WICKED SON

A WICKED SON BOOK
An Imprint of Post Hill Press
ISBN: 978-1-64293-584-4
ISBN (eBook): 978-1-64293-585-1

The Wrong Jew:
Defeating Those Who Want Us Dead
© 2021 by Hesh Kestin
All Rights Reserved

Post Hill Press
New York • Nashville
posthillpress.com

Published in the United States of America
1 2 3 4 5 6 7 8 9 10

FOR LEIGH

Adamantly sunny,
with unwavering fidelity
and the occasional threat
to shoot me in the head,
your valor roused mine
as for half a century
we crashed forward
through the brittle barriers
of mortal peril
and the commonplace,
two Wrong Jews.

Also by Hesh Kestin

Based on a True Story
The Iron Will of Shoeshine Cats
The Lie
The Siege of Tel Aviv

Table of Contents

Author's Preface

After "What's the book about?" the most common question authors must deal with is: "How did you come to write it?"

In the case of the book now in your hands, I'd much prefer the answer to be a joke: "Thirteen antisemites walk into a bar, followed by a Jewish publisher who changed his name from Schwartz, and then by a herd of feckless journalists." But in truth, *The Wrong Jew* came into being because all of the above walked not into a bar, but into my life…and changed it.

No joke. In April 2019, a normally well-thought-of publishing house brought out *The Siege of Tel Aviv*, my fourth work of fiction. What's *that* book about? (I thought you'd never ask.) For an answer, think of the bloody horror that would certainly ensue should Israel ever be overrun by its Islamist enemies. As Stephen King put it on the front cover: "Hesh Kestin's *The Siege of Tel Aviv* is scarier than anything Stephen King ever wrote— and then the fun begins as Israel fights back." He added: "This novel will cause talk and controversy. Most of all, it will be read."

With varying degrees of success, Steve has been generously recommending my novels to the public for a decade. Regarding controversy, he nailed it.

After thirteen tweets on the internet called *The Siege of Tel Aviv* "islamophobic" and "racist," its chicken-hearted publisher was so frightened by this antisemitic micro-mob, he recalled all the copies in bookstores and ordered them all pulped. The

Nazis preferred the bonfire. Then again, Hitler wasn't much of an environmentalist.

My sin: I had taken the Islamist universe at its word and described the tragedy of an Israeli defeat, where yet *another* six million Jews (yes, I know) are herded into Ghetto Tel Aviv to be wiped out, while once again the world sits on its hands thinking of what to order for lunch. Apparently, according to our thirteen twidiots, a Muslim victory would mean little more than every Jew in Israel being flown via magic carpet to Miami Beach—no bloodshed at all. Suggesting the bloody opposite was, therefore, islamophobic.

In point of fact, the only time I have had a phobic reaction to Muslims is when they have come bearing down on me in tanks. Other than that, as a soldier in the IDF, I have had the honor of serving twice under Arab commanders (one Muslim, one Christian). Via marriage, members of my family are Muslim. And as a former twenty-year resident of an Israeli village a stone's throw (perhaps there's a better term…) from the 1967 border known as the Green Line, many of my neighbors were Arabs. Poor things didn't know I was a racist so they kept inviting me to their homes for coffee and to their weddings for kabob and ear-splitting Arab music. If the Jew-haters who labeled me islamophobic on Twitter had actually read *The Siege of Tel Aviv*, they might have noticed that in it three Arab characters are downright heroes—well, in Israeli terms. I guess that wouldn't please them either.

We come now to our herd of feckless journalists. You'd think such defenders of free speech as *The New York Times, The Washington Post*, and *The Wall Street Journal* would have been all over a publisher who pulped his own book *because* it was selling well. Alas, despite my decades of personal and professional connections in journalism at the highest level, no one would touch the story. According to a friend at the *Times,* "They don't want to piss off the Arabs—running the story is too risky."

Perhaps worse, because reviews sell books: Though all my earlier prize-winning novels had been widely and positively reviewed, now…silence. Though within weeks after the pulping, I had digital and bound editions up for sale on Amazon (still there, still selling), though Stephen King was still recommending it, though it was anything if not timely…aside from a handful of positive notices, zip.*

When the dust settled it didn't take long to see the siege of *The Siege of Tel Aviv* as a metaphor for the horror story of what was happening in the world around me: Jew-hatred on the internet, gutless Jews like the former Schwartz cowering in fear, and the press—a good many of them Jews—and society in general unwilling to get involved.

The truth is my minor problem with Jew-hatred was as nothing compared to the antisemitic violence, verbal and ballistic, exploding across America. That the two are related is hardly a stretch: Antisemitism is a continuum—it starts with words, then desecration, then murder. Put simply, Islamists and white and black nationalists are on the march, encouraged by dog-whistle signals from scum at every level of government, shrugged off by a "neutral" press, and unopposed by Jews who either refuse to act or don't know how. What everyone believed was a post-Nazi paradise where Jews are safe has been shown to be little more than a universe of antisemitism in hiatus. Reborn less than a century

---

* Yet there were notable and laudable exceptions: Barbara Kay in Canada's *National Post*; Sheldon Teitelbaum in *Hadassah Magazine*; Aaron Leibel in *Washington Jewish Week*; fearless Muslim Maajid Nawaz on LBC radio in London; rising star Palestinian-American novelist Fawzy Zablah with a very fair review on the internet; and not least, a hard-charging piece in *Commentary* by Mark Horowitz.

after Jew-haters burned books, they have set out once again on the path to burn Jews.

One thing is certain: Turning our backs on those who would make Jews a target will no longer do. If we allow ourselves to be destroyed, they will destroy us.

—HK

Nota bene: Added up, hyphenated-Americans make up a majority of all Americans. By inference, if not outright example, some of the strategies outlined in this book may well serve as a guide for targeted minorities of all sorts. For those of our fellow victims who by happenstance read this book, I urge a bit of metaphysical editing: Whenever the phrase "the Wrong Jew" appears, it might be wise to read it as "the Wrong [fill in the blank]." We Jews are commanded to be a light unto the nations. In that light, much that is hidden may be revealed.

A Note on Sources

Curious, skeptical, or puzzled readers who would like further information on the sources of the facts, numbers, and quotes broadly distributed over the length of *The Wrong Jew* are invited to use Google or a similar search engine to verify their authenticity.

In most cases, the internet will deliver hundreds of citations testifying to same, but in one very critical situation it is often the case that statistics on dead and injured may vary from mine regarding victims of terrorism. This may be because: [a] Same-day news reports, which frequently lead the search engine listings, do not include the fact that an injured person had died from her wounds many weeks later; [b] Oddly, depending on the way the article is written, the number of victims of a terrorist act often do not include the deaths of police officers and civilians who brought the murderer down, this on the weird grounds such persons were not the terrorist's intended targets; [c] Perversely, news reports of the number of victims of a suicide bombing sometimes *include* the bomber—which suggests a mad twist on the old joke about the man who kills his parents and then asks the court for mercy on the grounds he is an orphan.

Yeah, I know. But as it happens, I spent a good part of my life as a journalist, in the Middle East and other bad neighborhoods, counting corpses. You would be surprised how often the official toll was four and the body count six. Still, should you discover a fault in the numbers, quotes, or facts that follow, please contact me at wrongjewbook@gmail.com. Upon verification, I will be pleased to attempt to update subsequent editions. As a general rule, it behooves all of us to heed the wise advice imparted during the early decades of the previous century to young reporters in Chicago: "If yer mama tells ya she loves ya, check it out."

*"In a place where
there are no men,
strive to be a man"*

–Hillel

Introduction

Entire libraries have been written about the causes of antisemitism, mostly because Jews have had an enormous lot of trouble figuring out why Christians, Muslims, and even Buddhists and animists, to say nothing of atheists, don't love us. (Agnostics simply don't know.) Jews are disliked where we live and where we don't, where we are a quarter of the population (as we were in mid-twentieth century New York City) and where there aren't enough in residence to field a couple of baseball teams. Japan is virtually *judenrein,* but manages to include Jews—second only to Koreans—in its demonology. And the Japanese really despise Koreans.

So let us be clear from the outset: The question this book sets out to answer is not why antisemites, but what to do about them. But first some definitions.

Jew. This is someone a second person sees as a Jew. Never mind that the Jew in question has morphed into a Methodist or a Buddhist. For all negative purposes, the essence of Judaism is not religious practice but genealogy, however adulterated by generations of intermarriage. Hitler's faithful servants sent people to their death at Auschwitz who had never seen the inside of a synagogue, knew no Hebrew, and whose dying wish was to be given absolution by a priest.

Goy. This Hebrew word simply means nation, as in all others. It is not in essence derogatory, except when used by those who have suffered at the hands of *goyim* (the plural) or whose sense of history goes back further than the last thirty seconds. In this book we will use *goy*, *goyim*, and *goyish* (this last the polar opposite of Jewish) sparingly but certainly not pejoratively.

Antisemitism. This is a societal disease whose bacillus creates antisemites, a broad category that includes everything from xenophobes, who are simply uncomfortably fearful around those who are different, to those who would exclude Jews from their towns and neighborhoods, to those who would exclude Jews from life itself. In its essence, antisemitism is social in nature. Though antisemitism can trip over itself—for instance, antisemites dislike Jews for being "clannish" and at the same for looking like, sounding like, and otherwise being like *goyim*—at its base, antisemitism is crystallized fear of the other when that other is a Jew. Often this is cloaked in religion—as expressed in the term Christ-killer—but one need hardly be a professor of divinity to realize that such dislike would likely have disappeared in the first century were it not for the parallel idea that such a grievous stain lasts eternally, that the family down the block is somehow responsible for the persecution and death of Jesus—and never mind that the Savior was himself a Jew. Still, antisemitism may be considered as only minimally toxic as any other spurious opinion until it manifests itself in action.

Jew-hatred. Ah, now we're getting somewhere. Jew-hatred is to antisemitism what lynching is to racism. Jew-hatred is not an opinion or a feeling. It is anything on the spectrum of planning to kill Jews to the actual act. It does not go too far to say that virulent Jew-hatred is largely dependent on opportunity. Give a Jew-hater a gun and an unguarded synagogue, and what was internal rage becomes murder. Give an unorganized group of Jew-haters a single identifiable Jew and a dark street, and the result will be the same. Permit a large number of Jew-haters to band together in an organization, and we have…

Nazism/nazism. Because we are speaking of varieties of political power, please note that this book will differentiate Nazis (card-holding members of the German National Socialist Party) from nazis (often called Neo-Nazis), those who would emulate Nazism's aims, but who are only loosely organized and not yet a political party. Think of Socialists and socialists: the former identifies a political party, the latter a set of ideas. In terms of identification, nazis may be white nationalists, black nationalists, Muslims, French super-patriots, or just plain nut jobs. Once antisemites become activists, they are nazis. Should they band together to form a political party, they may call themselves Nazis, or then again may be satisfied with such cloaking labels as Aryan Brotherhood. In brief, a nazi is someone who plans to hurt Jews.

Now that we have dealt with the problem of terminology, let us give the briefest of thoughts to understanding the reasons for antisemitism. This may best be explained by what at first glance appears to be a joke.

> Two Jews are walking down the street. Jerry is practically in tears. "Bob," he says, "I'm screwed. Unless I can get my hands on $32,500 by 10 AM tomorrow, I'm going to lose my business, my house, my kids will have to leave private school, and because of all this my wife will probably leave me. All because I can't get a hold of $32,500 by tomorrow morning."
>
> Just as Jerry finishes railing against fate, the two come upon a church. A large sign in front reads: *Today only: Become a Christian and get $32,500.* Jerry is transfixed.
>
> "Don't even think about it," Bob says.

"I'm not thinking one way or the other, but why shouldn't I go in and find out what this is all about?"

Bob begs him not to, but Jerry enters the church. An hour later, he returns to his friend, who asks what happened.

"Nothing much," Jerry says. "I met the priest, a very educated man, and we had a philosophical conversation, including a lot of stuff I never considered, and then I had a little bath. And that's it. I'm in. I'm a Christian. Nothing to it."

Bob: "But what about…"

"What about what?"

"What about the money? Did you get the money?"

Jerry fixes Bob with a hard look. "Don't you people," he says, "ever think about anything else?"

Okay, we have now completed our research into the reasons for antisemitism, which may best be summed up in the single scientific phrase, "Who gives a damn?"

Understanding antisemitism has classically been predicated on understanding ourselves: What are we doing wrong that has inspired otherwise nice *goyim* to hate us? This is as classically ass-backwards as anything can be. Number one: We're not talking here about nice *goyim*; we're talking about defective individuals acting both individually and as a group, but in both cases infected by the botulism of genetically-transmitted xenophobia—what is heard at the dinner table in one's youth is passed down as received truth in the next generation. In this it is really no different from perceptions of beauty and ugliness, or the idea that one must under no circumstances eat food that has fallen on the ground or swim within an hour after lunch. The difference between this type of groundless prejudice and hatred of another race, religion, or culture (alas, we're all three!) is that few people die because other people avoid black cats or believe the earth is flat. Such stupidity is victimless. It stops being victimless when it concerns negative misconceptions of other people as a group. "Those Jews can really belt out show tunes," is not quite the same as "All Jews think about is money."

Once this kind of opinion establishes itself in the body politic, it no longer makes sense to worry about why (Is it *us*? Nah, I don't recall having killed Christ this week), but what to do about *them*. After all, antisemitism can be expressed in anything from social snubs ("We can't permit you to live here") to homicide ("We can't permit you to live"). When we talk about antisemitism, we should be aware that we are not looking at an out-of-the-blue incident of Jew-hatred but at a continuum.

Antisemitism in all its forms is a fact of life. Trying to figure out the why of it normally—and perversely—leads to trying to figure out how to make people who hate Jews love us. Fuck. That. It has never worked. Assimilation? Nope. Giving to charity and supporting museums and concert halls? Nope. Setting up our own state where we won't be a minority? Double nope with a cherry on top. Rather than offer a shelter for Jews who are targets of hatred, the State of Israel serves as a lightning rod for the same. Instead of individual antisemites hating us, the establishment of the State of Israel is a convenient target of hatred not only by individuals but whole classes of people, to say nothing of whole countries.

Decried as racist by nations who are themselves racist as all get out—the UN in its mass wisdom confirmed that Zionism is racism—the Jewish State risked the lives of many white Israelis to bring to Zion over one hundred thousand black Jews from their native Ethiopia.

Gays as a class encourage the terrorists of Palestine, which executes homosexuals as a matter of law. And where is one of the world's largest annual gay rights parades? Tel Aviv.

Feminists look past the confounding brutality of the Muslim world toward women and condemn Israel for whatever else they can think up.

Democracies celebrate the enemies of an Israel that is the only democracy not only in the Middle East but in most of Africa and Asia.

The list is endless.

The solution to antisemitism is therefore not altering our behavior, but altering the behavior of those who would harm us. Pragmatically, viscerally, and—if it comes to that—violently.

This means becoming the Wrong Jew. As in, when they messed with him, they messed with the Wrong Jew.

It means putting aside defense and moving to offense. It means surgically removing from our DNA the gene for nice, the gene for playing fair, the gene for optimism, the gene for running away, the gene for thinking the monster who would slit our children's throats is just like us, only unenlightened, so let's have a productive dialogue to find common ground in order to resolve our differences. It means forgetting that we are liberal thinkers who will always respect others, even when those others plan to kill us. It means, as the Talmud has it, "If someone comes to kill you, rise up and kill him first."

Is preemptive war an effective approach? We have only to look at two wars which modern-day Israel fought within the same decade. In 1967, by going on the offensive, Israel defeated five Arab armies (and volunteers from as far away as Algeria and Cuba) in six days, with an Israeli death toll of eight hundred. In 1973, a surprise Pan-Arab attack cost an Israel playing defense thirty-five hundred fatalities, and damn near led to a second Holocaust.

The ultimate in Jewish Nice may be seen in three typical knee-jerk reactions to anti-Jewish violence:

1. Depend on the police. Surprise: These show up only after a crime has been committed.
2. But also post armed guards at the entrances of Jewish facilities, like synagogues and schools. Duh, same result: Guards outside are not able to distinguish between Jewish worshippers and their would-be killers. How would an armed guard know a Jew from a *goy*? Anyone can buy a skullcap. Anyone can smile and say "Shalom." The likelihood of an attacker showing up in full Nazi regalia is slim. Ah, but this is after all an *armed* guard. Really? How is a guard with a holstered gun going to defend the Jews under his protection if the nazi shoots him first?
3. Stand together. These are the clichéd bywords of our time. Somehow, Jews believe that by wearing cool tee-shirts and marching through the center of town, the evil-doers will melt away. Why? Because we're standing proudly together defying those who hate us by, uh, standing together, which signifies that we are a force to be dealt with because, uh, we are united in, uh, standing together.

Very well then, here is a brief history of Jews standing together. In the early 1930s, German Jews stood together in ignoring the rise of Nazism. In the late 1930s, German Jews stood together in wearing the yellow star and walking in the gutter because they were banned from the sidewalks, to say nothing of public parks and educational institutions from kindergarten through university. In a short time, German Jews would stand together on line for the trains that would deliver them to the death camps, where they would stand together on the way to showers raining poison gas. By the time Nazism had consolidated its power in Germany and Austria—because German Jews had stood together letting it happen when they had the money and manpower to fight back—Jews all over Nazi-conquered Europe and North Africa were standing together to be cut down by machine-gun fire and then, like their German-speaking coreligionists before them, standing together on the line to the ovens.

Standing together is what Nice Jews do. Fighting back is what Wrong Jews do.

In the last century, when the Nice Jews lined up to the slaughter, the Wrong Jews took to the forests with stolen weapons and fought; the Wrong Jews, many of them criminals (God bless them), fought back in the Warsaw Ghetto. When Israel was threatened by an Arab naval blockade, the Wrong Jews launched what would become the Six-Day War. When Syria and Iraq were found to be working on nuclear bombs, the Wrong Jews bombed their facilities. When Arab terrorists attacked Jews in Europe, Israel's Wrong Jews opened a terror front against them, wiping out an entire generation of killers by killing them first.

The lesson is as simple as it is existential. Mess with us, even think of it, and we will wipe you out. Why? Because we can no longer afford the luxury of being the Nice Jews of tradition. We must be the Wrong Jews of today.

Otherwise, there will not be Jews of any sort tomorrow.

CHAPTER 1

— ✡ —

Understanding the Threat

I n order to combat antisemites, it makes sense to separate the real threats from the noise.

Item: A newly elected Democratic member of Congress, Somalia-born Muslim Ilhan Omar, drops anti-Israel, antisemitic tropes the way an earlier generation of politicians promised to fight godless Communism, and for the same reason: to stoke the ambient fear of a specific demographic given to xenophobia. It hardly matters whether Rep. Omar actually believes Jews secretly hold the levers of power around the world, or whether Jews are only interested in "the benjamins"—slang for one hundred dollar bills—because the upshot is the same: An attack on Jews from the elected political left that could be mistaken for something Stalin was likely to utter before breakfast on the day in 1953 he ordered the arrest of Jewish doctors for conspiring to poison the Soviet leadership.

Item: Across the country, university student bodies, goaded by a professoriate whose job security is guaranteed by the most rigid tenure, have turned college campuses into no-go areas for pro-Israeli and Jewish groups, and in many cases for individual Jews. The tide of antisemitic political correctness has risen so high that President Donald Trump, himself more than once accused of antisemitic statements, in 2019 signed an executive order that includes antisemitic activities and the "targeting of the State of Israel" under Title VI of the Civil Rights Act, which bars discrimination on the basis of race, color, and national origin at colleges and universities that receive federal funding.

Item: The organizers of marches for transsexual and gay rights so automatically align themselves with the Palestinian cause that fellow left-wingers are forbidden to display signs of Jewish affiliation. Never mind that gays are regularly executed by the PLO and in Gaza, in fact in most of the Muslim world, and that the only trans in the Arab Middle East is the state formerly known as Trans-Jordan, which dropped the prefix in 1949.

Item: Recent years have witnessed an explosion of deadly violence against Jews. In 2018, a right-wing fanatic walked into Tree of Life Synagogue in Pittsburgh and killed eleven worshippers at Sabbath services. Exactly six months later, another right-wing fanatic walked into the Chabad of Poway Synagogue in Southern California and opened fire on the congregants at prayer on the final day of Passover, killing one worshipper and wounding three others before his rifle jammed.

Question: Which side of the Jew-hatred compass is most threatening to Jewish life—not the quality of Jewish life, but Jewish life itself? Yes, arguably, the so-called Progressive wing of the Democratic Party (and groups further to the left) has made life uncomfortable for many Jews, but so far, these unreconstructed lefties have not taken one Jewish life. Their actions are limited to words.

The right wing, or nazi, side of Jew-hatred is accountable for having taken at least twelve lives in the two years prior to 2020. We're not bothering to count desecration of cemeteries, swastikas decorating synagogue walls, and the near surreal riot of nazis in Charlottesville, Virginia where an estimated five hundred to six hundred white supremacists, a good many armed, marched against a counter-demonstration that resulted in the death of a thirty-two-year-old woman run down by an automobile driven by a nazi. If you've forgotten what those nazis were shouting, it was "Jews will not replace us." Okay, the idea that Jews are trying to replace fascist white-supremacists makes no sense, but that's just a problem for the syntactically challenged. What they meant to say is: "Jews will not replace white people."

Despite the occasional harassment of Jews in Brooklyn's Crown Heights neighborhood, where black-of-hat *hasidim* live cheek by jowl with their black-of-skin neighbors, the resultant strife is related less to left-wing antisemitism than to inter-group rivalry, if not outright enmity. The vociferously antisemitic national left has shown itself to be ideologically and politically malevolent, but so far has not caused the loss of one Jewish life.

Which means, for the present, Jews are threatened *existentially* only by nazis.

The threat from the left may one day transmogrify into violence, but it is clear that white supremacists are the enemy *du jour*. This distinction is important because knowing one's enemy is essential to combatting him. That is especially true when the media noise seems to concentrate on Progressive antisemitism, as spoken in Congress or tweeted by its members, and used by the left—in socio-political organizations and on college campuses—to exclude differences of opinion about Jews and especially Israel by the simple tactic of excluding Jews and Israelis. Hearing through this left-wing noise to the sound of guns being cocked in the hands of nazis is a bit like making out a single

French horn from within a symphony orchestra. But listen hard. It's there.

This parallels the distinction Israel has learned to make regarding the motivations of its enemies. While it was long supposed the issue was one of real estate—who has rights to the land of Israel?—over the years it has now become clear the dispute is religious, certainly on the part of the Muslim world and, though somewhat attenuated, on the Israeli side as well. The difference is that Israel has long taken a pragmatic approach that assumed a compromise could be cobbled together, the by now infamous land-for-peace argument that sharing the land would end the bloodshed of a century.

But it turns out the Muslim argument is not about something that can be debated or negotiated. It is about "God's will." According to the Koran, land once ruled by Muslims may be not be possessed by the infidel. This applies to the Christian infidel as well: Were they able to take it back, Islam would be pointing its guns at the Iberian Peninsula—and in one major attack in 2004 succeeded in killing 193 people and injuring 2,000 in coordinated bombings on Madrid's commuter train network. It is not clear why there were no further major attacks, other than an even greater loathing for the Jewish State (the little Satan) and the US (the big Satan). Israel is not only planted in the heart of the Arab world, but Israel's very capital is in what the Muslim world calls *Al Kuds*, site of the Al-Aqsa Mosque and the Dome of the Rock, among the most venerated sites in Islam.

As Muslims have become more and more Islamist—that is to say, more politically religious—it's become abundantly clear to Israel that compromise is a western idea that cannot be made to fit an absolutist faith. So why bother trying?

There are clear parallels here with the underpinnings of nazism: White/Christian supremacy is absolutist. Think of it: a tiny drop of non-Aryan blood serves to invalidate the humanity of any individual. Similarly, Islam will not give up one inch of territory to the infidel. It is the total negation of the other that makes both so dangerous: Once Jews are understood to be monsters or animals—lice, rats, snakes, an entire fauna of inhumanity—then killing them off, killing us off, becomes perfectly logical.

It also means there is no sense in debating the issue. There are, in fact, only three conceivable Jewish reactions: (1) Ignore the attacks in the hope they will go away; (2) defend against them; (3) destroy those who would destroy us. Let's examine each.

(1) To a certain extent, benign neglect is theoretically a valid response. There are crazy people everywhere and of every ideological and political stripe. Pragmatically, making a big deal out of one or two lunatics may be seen as counter-productive because, in theory, this would serve only to give their ideas platform in the sense of publicity and validity. That a few people seriously believe smoking prevents cancer or that space aliens walk among us keeps us from debating the very real issues of our time, and can be said to hijack the spotlight in the public arena. Red herrings should indeed be ignored. But when it comes to red sharks, we must be more wary. No one has ever been eaten by a herring.

Ignore and hope it will go away was in fact one of the keys to the rise of Nazism in Europe. In the early 1930s, this was the attitude of Germany's Jewish community, whose political, social, and financial leadership saw no threat in the foaming at the mouth statements of the nascent National Socialists; some Jews even supported the Nazis financially to counterbalance the growth of German Communism.

At this point, we must question how much could have been done by Germany's Jews, cultured people whose hands would remain clean until the day they were forced to scrub the streets of Berlin and German-controlled Vienna with toothbrushes as their Nazi neighbors cheered.

By 1930, Jews made up an astounding percentage of Germany's *feinschmeckers*, its elevated connoisseur class, its intellectuals, doctors, lawyers, business leaders; its wealthy and refined. These people were not going to go out and battle Nazis in the street, nor as capitalists were they going to support those who would, the Communists. So, they sat on their clean hands until four hundred Nazis grew into forty thousand and then forty million. Of course, the Nazis were not sitting on their hands. To an incalculable extent, they fueled their drive to power with money and property seized from the very Jews who had snubbed fighting them. It is not a stretch to say the murder of six million Jews and some five million Gypsies, Socialists, and Communists, and the mentally and physically disabled, may at least partially be derived from the irresponsibility of German Jewry in looking the other way.

(2) Thus, defending against acts of violence would appear to be a decent alternative to doing nothing. But as any corporal will affirm, defense is a poor path to victory. France's storied Maginot Line was easily penetrated by German tanks; the Bar-Lev string of fortifications Israel built on the shores of the Suez Canal hardly prevented the Egyptians from crossing into Sinai in the Yom Kippur War. Anyone who has ever been physically attacked will tell you that rolling into a ball is not going to disarm your attacker.

And in practical terms, there is no way to defend against nazi violence. Hire armed guards to protect the front door of your synagogue? What happens when that initial protection is overcome? Should our children be at risk of attack in the public schools—in these times, private schools as well—why not enroll them in Jewish schools? Do that and you will provide an even better target for those who would murder Jewish children. The simple truth is that there is no adequate defense against dedicated attackers, only the semblance of defense, the illusion of safety. Perhaps worse, such fantasizing carries an opportunity cost: When we invest time, effort, and funds on defense, we neglect the only real protection, which is going on the offensive.

(3) The question is, how does a community of American *feinschmeckers* do that? And Jews in America are the precise equivalent of German Jews of the last century in their reluctance to get their hands dirty. Just as German Jews felt German, many having fought for the fatherland in World War II, American Jews have up to now felt unqualifiedly American, with no need to consider self-defense. Since Hitler's defeat, we have had the idea that violent antisemitism would never again raise its ugly head, in which case a strategy for survival is unnecessary.

But it has. And it is.

Which is why this little book will lay out a battle plan for our physical survival in a venomous social and political environment. As such, it may well be ignored by an American Jewry which has chosen a more dignified path, which path, if things go badly, may lead to the literal death of American Jewry, and certainly to the death of many American Jews.

CHAPTER 2

✡

What We Are Up Against

As it happens, I am one of a small number of Jews whose existential DNA is equally American and Israeli. Born and raised in New York, at the age of twenty-six, I and my new bride made our way to Jerusalem with the avowed intention of becoming citizens of Israel, where we lived for twenty years. Our five children were born in Israel. As a journalist, I made my living in Israel (and on the side worked an orange grove, which is almost laughably old-time Israeli). Leigh, who had been a ballerina in Houston, where she grew up, and in New York, where we met, established herself as a teacher of ballet in the then small village of Karkur, where we lived in a farmhouse suffused with the aroma of thousands of citrus trees, mine and my neighbors'.

Over a period of some eighteen years in which I served in the reserves of the Israel Defense Forces, I was in uniform for a total of some six years, a good deal of that time in war, serving as a battle medic in a reconnaissance platoon. And temporarily elevated in rank, I was for a limited time deployed to liaison with the officialdom of the various UN forces on Israel's borders; I suspect I got the assignment because, unlike most Israeli officers, I was, at least then, able to hold my liquor. It doesn't get more liaison than that. Though tens of thousands of idealistic diaspora Jews have turned up in Israel committed to make it in the new old country, the vast majority leave after a few years, sometimes months, when it becomes clear that living under threat of annihilation in a society that demands a certain thickness of skin, and usually offers a corresponding thinness of income, just ain't for them.

It is hard to blame them, but then again most did not have the advantages I had. My father was a Zionist organizer in the Polish village in which he'd been raised, arriving in America as a refugee in 1939, having fled Warsaw only days before the Wehrmacht swept in. He was fortunate in having secured a US entry visa at a time when the British did not permit European Jews to find shelter in Mandate Palestine. Though he became a grateful and proud American, like the medieval Jewish poet Yehuda HaLevi, his heart was in the east while the rest of him remained in the west. For me, the turning point came during the Six-Day War of 1967, when I was a reporter for *Newsday*, a large New York area newspaper.

I was all of twenty-three, the youngest reporter on staff, detailed to cover what was at first the civil rights movement and then its rather less pacific transmogrification into Black Power. By May of that year, I was convinced war would be breaking out in the Middle East. Egypt had closed the Suez Canal and the Straits of Tiran to Israeli shipping and had signed an agreement of military cooperation with Israel's other neighbors, Syria and Jordan.

I'd grown up in a rough neighborhood in Brooklyn where it was common to be ganged up on; I could see it coming. So, I applied for a passport with the brash intention of cabling my editors from Jerusalem when hostilities broke out to tell them their Mideast war correspondent was in place. A great plan, except that on June 5th the war broke out—and I had no passport.

Stewing at my bad luck—I might have had worse luck as a virgin war correspondent who didn't know a flanking maneuver from *flanken*—on the third day of war, when it appeared Israel was on its way to victory, my editor introduced me to a Mexican journalist on a fellowship who was to accompany me along with a photographer to report on how New York's Jewish community was taking the news.

To say there was joy aplenty is to understate the euphoria, but what struck me was its peculiar form. Religious and secular, old and young, male and female, all repeated in almost the same phrasing the same shameless boast: "We really beat the shit out of those Arabs," or "We really taught them Arabs a lesson." That first-person plural began as a small irritation, and after endless repetition, became an open sore. Who was this *we*? We? We?! This wasn't the Mets winning the World Series, this was war. Some eight hundred Israelis died in their helmets and combat boots, not baseball caps and sneakers; no fewer than twenty-five hundred were wounded, many crippled for life. What sort of chutzpa permitted New York's Jewish shopkeepers, doctors, accountants, housewives, taxi-drivers, and lawyers to hitch a ride on the blood and sweat of Israelis who had put their lives on the line and were indeed that very day still dying in the process?

Even worse, I was compelled to explain this phenomenon to my tag-along Mexican journalist, who had a bit of trouble getting his head around the same question. I do recall leaving some note of this bizarre situation in the article I wrote later that day, and I recall as well my displeasure the next morning when I saw it had been edited out. No matter, I had already resolved to ascend to Israel and, in joining the Israel Defense Forces (IDF), assume the risks of Israeli citizenship as well as the rewards.

In the years after my return to America in 1990, I would be embarrassed to hear North American Jewry take credit for Israel's accomplishments on the battlefield: Not only were American Jews prepared to fight to the last Israeli (Israel's combat fatalities since the War of Independence are estimated at over twenty-four thousand), but few had any feelings for the dead and their families among our enemies (some eighty-six thousand), most of the latter unwilling conscripts in political wars they barely understood. According to the Talmud, God silenced the angels who were about to break into song on seeing the Egyptians drowning in the Red Sea, declaring, "How dare you sing for joy when My creatures are dying!"

Equally repugnant, if not more so, are those stainless diaspora Jews who find Israel to be morally corrupt in, say, building a wall to keep out terrorists, or bombing buildings in Gaza where the terror infrastructure uses hapless civilians as a shield. Put plainly, if it's not your life in danger, kindly don't lecture Israelis on how to protect themselves.

For me, it didn't take long to realize what sort of Jew I was.

In 1974, having been demobilized after the Yom Kippur War, I found myself in New York on a magazine assignment. I was on my way to find a shop that sold mini-tape recorders to document my interviews when, in an alcove formed by the plywood walls surrounding a construction site, I spotted a young man behind a makeshift table on which were displayed…mini-tape recorders. When I picked one up to check it out, he came out from behind his table and asked me in soft Egyptian-toned Arabic if I were an Arab. I smiled and replied in minimal Arabic, "No, a Jew." And there, as hundreds of New Yorkers flowed by, many of them my co-religionists, we two enemies, survivors of the same war, embraced. In the three years since my ascendance to Israel, I had grown to have more in common with my enemies than with the Jews I had grown up with, even with members of my American family.

The tape recorder I bought that day was to work for a long time, during which period it became more clear that American Jews were so dependent on Israel not only out of pride but out of a sense of their own lack of agency. One did not have to look too far back in Jewish history to see the contrast between the impotence of diaspora Jewry, its near total inability to take charge of its own fate, compared to the virility of their brothers and cousins in establishing and maintaining a vibrant Jewish state. Fertility rate comparisons are telling: Israeli Jews are fecund, with a birthrate of 3.09, the highest in the developed world; American Jews are existentially barren, with a birthrate half of Israel's, far below replacement level.

It is this lack of agency among US Jews that is most concerning in the present crisis. When it is all boiled down, American Jewry appears to be unwilling to pay the price of our continued existence. Even at the peak of our electoral power, the forties and fifties, a time when our votes were powerfully concentrated in a number of Congressional districts, when it came to exercising that power to save the Jews of Europe, America's Jewish leadership displayed little more than fear and trembling.

It has not gotten better. Though Jewish votes might make or break a presidential campaign, and though Jewish money was and remains key to electoral success at every level of government, with the exception of support for Israel, Jews have been reluctant to stand up as a political force. By contrast, Afro-American leaders have used their community's power at the ballot box to press their demands, as in recent years have the leaders of Latino communities from California to Florida. There is *Black Power* and *Latino Power*, but no one marches under the banner of *Jewish*

Power. We need look no further than the total abdication of responsibility to their own community in the silence of American Jewish leaders (and Jews broadly) when President Trump chillingly whitewashed the homegrown nazis who hate-marched by the hundreds in 2018 against Jews in Charlottesville, Virginia. That Trump said "There are very fine people on both sides," is not the point; he was merely speaking to his know-nothing base. That this did not cause American Jewish leaders to come together in vociferous complaint is.

Don't Jewish lives matter?

Partially the problem is in the nature of our Jewish leadership, which we'll examine later, but at base what we have here is the same sort of head-in-the-sand passivity that the Jews of Germany exhibited at the dawn of the Nazi era: (a) Let's not give anyone reasons to dislike us even more than they do now; (b) We're busy with our private lives; (c) Likely this is an aberration that will soon blow over; and (d) Surely when Trump said there are good nazis, he didn't mean it or was simply his usual slop-speaking self.

It used to be a subject of dinner party conversation: Who has it worse—men or women? But since no one can claim to have been both, the subject is essentially unsettleable, not even by novelists able to invent characters who are, sequentially, both. What's the relevance? I haven't been both genders, but I have been both nationalities, and I can tell you a lot more than you'd probably like to hear about the distinctive differences between these two groups which more or less split between them the world's nearly fifteen million Jews.

American and Israeli Jews are not much different in matters of relative income, class, religion, national origin, or political leanings. The singular distinction between them is that when the chips are down, Israelis are prepared to fight those who would annihilate them; from all indications, their American cousins are prepared to be annihilated.

Israelis are ready to put their lives at risk in the IDF; American Jews, who had a distinguished record in the armed forces in World War II, as a group remained civilians during the Korean Conflict, the Vietnam War, and America's longest war, that against Jew-hating Islamist terror, in Iraq and Afghanistan. Not for nothing have the Jewish neo-conservatives who pressed for the war on terror been characterized as chicken hawks. Almost none have shouldered weapons, and neither have their children.

In this, their absence is consonant with the American gentile upper class with whom they identify. The last American president whose child served in the armed forces was George H. W. Bush, and "W" never left the US; the last president whose child served in combat was Dwight D. Eisenhower. Instead, America's leaders have sent others to fight a series of three unwinnable wars in Vietnam, Afghanistan, and Iraq.

Show me an American Jewish family and I will show you a superciliously brazen disregard for the honor of arms. Grandpa Sam may have landed at Omaha Beach, but his descendants are content to wade ashore following an invigorating swim in the clear blue waters of St. Barts or Anguilla. The single most threatened American minority—by unit of population—is the least likely to own a gun. The young cohort of this minority are more likely to take tennis than karate lessons.

Israeli Jews are by comparison a different species. No matter their politics, Israelis are willing to put their lives on the line to protect their families, their homes, their nation. No matter their politics, American Jews are willing to fight to the last *goy* when it comes to the country that has given them religious and political freedom, unlimited opportunity, and enormous wealth.

Unlike those who have no way to compare the lives of men and women, I have been both an American Jew and an Israeli

Jew. American Jews have drunk the kosher Kool-Aid that armed guards, police, and the law will protect them. In the process, we have become soft, malleable, even uninterested in the world that threatens to come crashing down on us. Israelis have no such choice. It can be said of Israelis that when the Arabs targeted them for destruction, they picked on the Wrong Jews. It can equally well be said of American Jews that when nazis targeted (and target!) them for destruction, they picked on the right Jews.

It is time American Jews became the Wrong Jews. But words alone will not create everyday heroes. We must do it ourselves.

CHAPTER 3

Fashions in Jew-Hatred

As I write this, six people are dead in Jersey City following an attack on a kosher grocery by black antisemites calling themselves Black Hebrew Israelites—an eerie echo of the 2015 attack by Muslim antisemites on a kosher grocery in Paris that left four dead. As a former foreign correspondent specializing in terrorism, it is not unexpected that I have had a good deal of contact over the years with Islamists. But as it happens, I also have connections with both antisemitism in Jersey City and these same Black Hebrew Israelites.

The first occurred when I was all of four years old. My father, Bernard Louis Kestin, operated a delicatessen cum liquor store in the then déclassé streets just off Journal Square, the epicenter of a run-down city whose population was at the time composed mainly of first-generation Americans with Polish, Italian, and Irish surnames. At four, I was hardly aware of the ethnic identities of my tormentors; I recall only confusion at being surrounded by a gang of older boys who kept calling me "Christ killer." I do recall it was the dead of winter and that they were, more or less successfully, attempting to strip me of my clothes (ostensibly to examine a bit of my physiognomy that differed from theirs) when my father came out of the store and saved me.

Some twenty years later, when I was a magazine editor living on the then raffish Upper West Side—now anything but—I was working from home when a tall, thin black messenger knocked on my door on West 70th Street to deliver a manuscript. He was dressed to impress in the kind of Africa drag then sold in Harlem: Garishly striped dashiki accentuated with gold thread, a boubou cap on his head, and carrying what he called his "ma'-keh," close enough to the Hebrew for stick, elaborately carved and about four feet long. I engaged him in conversation long enough to learn he was a Black Hebrew Israelite, that my own people were not authentic Jews but Edomites (that is, nationals of a biblical neighbor of Canaan) who had usurped the identity of the "original black Jews," and that one day justice would be done to us—which I understood to mean me. (Let's not confuse the Black Hebrew Israelites with authentic black Jews, either those who are the product of mixed marriage or those who have chosen to convert to Judaism. The Black Hebrew Israelites are a sect, as unrelated to normative Judaism as Jews for Jesus or Jews from Mars.)

Pretty damn quick, I ended the conversation, sent him on his way, and some years later learned that a group of some five thousand Black Hebrew Israelites had found their way to Israel in the late sixties on tourist visas, which they overstayed. The entire community settled as squatters in empty apartments in Dimona, a down-at-the-heels town in the Negev desert. Eventually Jerusalem, frustrated to have within its borders another population that challenged Jewish rights to the Holy Land, tried to deport the group back to the US. Eventually, through pressure on Jerusalem from the Congressional Black Caucus—alas, there is no Congressional Jewish Caucus—they have been granted permanent residency status. According to press reports, some serve in the IDF; one is a member of the Dimona city council.

So here, in the experience of one Jew, are contacts with traditional antisemites—poor white Catholics who had absorbed hatred of Jews from their parents and from the nuns and priests responsible for their education—and a bizarrely perverse iteration of Jew-hatred by blacks who have managed to conflate themselves with traditional Jews in the sense of feeling persecuted. In essence, they claim that normative Jews are not the real victims of antisemitism, we are—and you, who call yourselves Jews, have stolen our identity and the honorable mantle of being hated. So we hate *you*.

Of course I've also had the wonderful experiences of several other sources of antisemitism:

1. I'm a veteran of two wars (and a number of exchanges of live fire which no one bothered to classify as anything more than incidents) and, as a correspondent, witness to the result of many fatal attacks on Israeli civilians—if that's not antisemitism, then the entire opus of Arab nationalism is somehow an illusion.

2. I've met dozens, if not hundreds, of white American and European antisemites whose shtick is to disavow hatred of Jews while declaiming on the evil of Zionism, Zionists, Israelis, and Israel. Perhaps the single great exemplar of this sleight-of-hand Jew-hatred is Jeremy Corbyn, now stepped down as leader of the Labour Party in the UK. A poll by *The Jewish Chronicle* found that 87 percent of British Jews found Corbyn to be "personally antisemitic." Apparently,

the other 13 percent have been asleep since 2015, when he began making over Labour in his own image.

But personal experience hardly begins to outline the styles, if not fashions, in international antisemitism. Speaking generally, here are some but not all of the principal models of Jew-hatred, how they differ, and how they do not.

(a) **The Nazi model.** This places Jews in the basket we'll call sub-human, which very conveniently permitted and encouraged Germany and its various European henchmen to treat Jews as both a race (condemning to death even those who had generations earlier converted to Christianity) and as a religion (so that converts to Judaism faced the same fate). Not only did the Nazi model make no distinction between genealogy and faith, but in fact managed to infuse both with nationality, a notion that would have delighted Theodor Herzl; except that in the German-version, Jews, Judaism, and even Jewishness, whatever that is, were treated as an alien and—*ipso facto*—inhuman strain.

(b) **The French model.** Though Napoleon was greeted by the Jews of the lands he conquered as a liberator (sometimes *the* Messiah, according to tradition an executive position for which there is no religious or ethnic qualification) because he gave full rights of citizenship to the Jews of France as well as those of the Napoleonic Empire, France before, during, and after the new emperor was and remains a hotbed of antisemitism. In *la belle France* it is a matter of *la belle religion propre établie*.

Despite the French Revolution, despite Napoleon, and against reasonable expectations, the established religion of France is a Roman Catholicism that in its attitude to Jews is surpassed only by Poland's, where hatred of Jews remains a subject of instruction from the pulpit at mass. In 2019, the Polish government gained kudos abroad and criticism at home for arresting one Jacek Miedlar on a charge of public incitement against

Jews. Miedlar, who called Jews a cancer, is a former priest, who would have been above the law wearing the cassock.

The 1894 treason conviction of Alfred Dreyfus, a Jewish artillery colonel, on fabricated evidence may be viewed as a perfectly refined example of French antisemitism. *L'affaire Dreyfus* came about in an era where *La Libre Parole*, an antisemitic newspaper, had a circulation of three hundred thousand, mainly in Paris (it lasted from 1892 to 1924). It almost certainly would not have happened had Col. Dreyfus been a convert to Catholicism: Jews then and now pass easily into the sunlight of acceptance once they are baptized. Nothing better illustrates this than the case of Jean-Marie Lustiger, who shocked his Jewish parents by converting to Catholicism at age fourteen. Eventually, he became Archbishop of Paris, and for a time stood a fair chance of being elected Pope. In keeping with his belief that he was a Jew who had found Christ, Lustiger's 2007 funeral at Notre Dame was preceded by the recital of *Kaddish*. The French model is at once far more open and closed than others, reflecting the ambivalence of French society in general: Become Catholic, speak perfect French, know the difference between a Viognier and a Sauvignon blanc, and *ipso facto* you are no longer a Jew.

(c) **The British model.** Crossing the English Channel, one enters into another world of antisemitism, one which is cultural in the extreme. Like everything else in British society, its style is denominated according to a rigid system that excludes Jews, Muslims, and even Her Majesty's subjects who are not English. When Anita Roddick, founder of The Body Shop, made the point that her products underwent "no animal testing," she was asked if products were actually tested; She is said to have replied: "Certainly, on the Welsh."

In polite English society, Judaism remains a genealogic stain that may not be removed by baptism. Benjamin Disraeli, who was prime minister in 1868 and again from 1874 to 1880, was reviled as a Jew despite his baptism in the Church of England. Disraeli was also one of the most popular novelists of his time, whose fiction was replete with Jewish stereotypes. Eugen Karl Dühring, a major anti-Jewish theorist in Germany, subscribed to Disraeli's racial doctrine: "The Jews are to be defined solely on the basis of race," he wrote, "And not on the basis of religion." Hitler was a fan.

The persistence of cultural antisemitism on the British right is a bottomless pit, and here I am not speaking of ancient history:

A few months before the 2001 general election in which he first entered Parliament as a Conservative, the editor of *The Spectator* published an article by the exuberantly racist columnist who wrote as "Taki," (which—spelling slightly altered—he was). The article confirmed his belief in a Jewish world conspiracy and declared himself to be a "*soi-disant* anti-Semite." Despite protestations by the magazine's owner, Conrad Black, Taki was not sacked. *The Spectator*'s editor at the time? One Boris Johnson, now prime minister of the United Kingdom.

In October 2004, *Guardian* journalist Simon Hoggart reported a leading Conservative Party politician saying, "The trouble is that the party is being run by Michael Howard, Maurice Saatchi, and Oliver Letwin—and none of them really knows what it is to be English." Howard, Saatchi, and Letwin? All Jews.

In Tory circles, it starts early: In 2011, an officer of the Oxford University Conservative Association stated that members at weekly meetings were wont to sing a Nazi-themed song that included the lines "Dashing through the Reich / killing lots of Kike."

As recently as 2020, John Bercow, upon ending his tenure as Speaker of the House of Commons, told *The Sunday Times*, "I did experience antisemitism from members of [my own] Conservative Party.... A lot was subtle. I remember a member saying, 'If I had my way, Ber*koff*, people like you wouldn't be allowed in this place.'" Though by tradition, retiring Commons Speakers are elevated to the House of Lords, for Bercow this did not happen.

That's a taste of the Tory side of the antisemitic menu. For those of us who have come to believe that Labour's defamation of individual Jews, Jews in general, and Israel twenty-four seven somehow began with Jeremy Corbyn's ascendance in the British left, the historical record is full of evidence to the contrary. Labour, which attracted many Jews, had its own style:

As European correspondent for *Forbes*, I had the dubious pleasure of spending several hours with Robert Maxwell at his offices at *The Daily Mirror*, where in the middle of our conversation I baited the press lord by casually dropping in a question in Yiddish. I suspected this was Maxwell's first language, though up until then, the press lord had hidden his origins as the son of Jewish parents in what is now Ukraine. Without missing a beat, Maxwell pretended not to have heard and continued jauntily on in the plummy tones of the English upper class. A couple of years later, it happened that my good friend the late Arthur Davidson, QC, a former Labour member of Parliament from a largely non-Jewish constituency, was at the time Maxwell's lawyer. He too took pains to gloss over his Jewish background, though he admitted it to me while hiding out from Maxwell at our home in the Hamptons: it seemed Maxwell would phone him day and night—he needed a break.

That these two Jewish former Labour MPs masqueraded as *goyim* indicates the level of anti-Jewish feeling in Labour, though this is now disguised, rather poorly, as anti-Zionism. Labour leader Jeremy Corbyn could barely open his mouth without spewing disapproval of the very existence of British Jewry. A YouGov poll commissioned by the Campaign Against Antisemitism (CAA) found that 67 percent of British adults who strongly support UK Labour leader Jeremy Corbyn "hold at least one antisemitic view." In a forward to the study, Gideon Falter, founder of the CAA, wrote that "Antisemitism on the far-left now exceeds antisemitism on the far-right."

So, it's a competition then?

Whichever party wins, it's clear that from both sides of the aisle, the UK's leadership, as well as its rank and file, exhibit the same tendency to revile Jews for not being sufficiently British. As one British politician said, "They may be British, but they'll never be English." In other words, a UK passport is just not enough when it comes to cultural identity.

To this day, British society remains antisemitic in a way distinct from that of the variety just across the English Channel. In France, one might cleanse the stain of one's Judaism by becoming "French" in culture, religion, and even speech. In Britain, this has proven impossible. When Maxwell's first bid to buy an English daily failed, *The News of the World*'s editor ran a front-page piece explaining the paper's refusal to sell: "This is a British paper, run by British people…as British as roast beef and Yorkshire Pudding…. Let us keep it that way."

Beyond the public history, I offer this reminiscence from the Kestin family archives. In the late 1980s, my wife and our (then) four children lived in the rather posh London neighborhood of Holland Park. Our youngest, Ketura, was in nursery school; Ross, then eight, was in the neighborhood elementary, Fox School, one of the city's best; and the older kids, fifteen year-old Margalit and Ari, twelve, were in Holland Park Comprehensive. What we didn't know was that upon graduation, Fox pupils were routinely enrolled in private schools, leaving Holland Park virtually empty of neighborhood students. The result: Kids from London's poorer areas were bussed in to fill Holland Park Comprehensive. Further result: When our older kids were discovered to be Jews by their classmates, violence on a daily basis ensued. Margalit had her head smashed into a concrete wall by a gang of girls; Ari fought off young Jew-haters regularly as a matter of course. Their tormentors were likely the Labour Party of the coming decades. As to the school administrators, these likely voted for the Conservative Party: They could or would do nothing. What we did was send the kids back to school in Israel. We followed soon after.

(d) **The Islamic model.** Where to begin? The Arab riots of 1929 that wiped out the Jewish community of Hebron that had existed before the birth of Mohammed? The Grand Mufti of Jerusalem rushing to Berlin to propose to Hitler the recruitment of Arab divisions for the Wehrmacht? The combined Islamic attack in 1948 on the newly declared State of Israel, which drew Muslims from as far away as Pakistan and Morocco? The schoolbooks printed by the Palestine Liberation Organization (and paid for by the UN, mostly with American funding) that feature caricatures of long-nosed, saliva-dripping murderous Jews?

For me, it began with a simple statement by my Polish-born father, whose political sophistication was second to no one's, when as we listened to the news on the kitchen radio of Egyptian dictator Gamal Abdel Nasser's incendiary rhetoric in the 1950s, he muttered in Yiddish: "*An antisemit a greyser.*" Seeing through what was then and is even now considered to be a mere real estate dispute, he nailed it: "One big antisemite."

The old man was even then aware that hatred of Israel, with its coda of throwing all Israelis into the sea, was simply hatred of Jews in concentrated form. Founded to free Jews from hatred, the Jewish State has instead become a magnet for same, not only by individuals around the world but by its nations. Earlier I mentioned the UN's 1975 declaration that Zionism is Racism. For the record, the vote was 72 for, 39 against, with 32 abstaining. Among the countries in favor were such paragons of racial and religious equality as Afghanistan, Algeria,

Bangladesh, China, Congo, Cuba, Egypt, South Yemen, Egypt, India, Indonesia, Iran, Iraq, Jordan, Cambodia, Kuwait, Libya, Malaysia, Nigeria, Oman, Pakistan, Poland, Qatar, Rwanda, Saudi Arabia, Sri Lanka, Sudan, Syria, Turkey, the United Arab Emirates, and Yemen. Most of these remain proud of attempting to kill off their minorities.

Before tearing up the text of that resolution from the podium of the General Assembly, Chaim Herzog, Israel's envoy to the world body, noted the irony that "it is as natural for an Arab to serve in public office in Israel as it is incongruous to think of a Jew serving in any public office in an Arab country, indeed being admitted to many of them." As it happens, the former head of Israel's electoral commission is retired Supreme Court justice Salim Joubran, an Arab Israeli; as is Dr. Samer Haj Yehia, the first Muslim to become chairman of a major Israeli bank, in this case the nation's oldest and largest, Bank Leumi, which was founded with funds collected by none other than Theodor Herzl.

That Arabs, Muslim and Christian, along with Druse, have risen to leadership levels in Israel hardly bothers the Arab nations who continue an antisemitic tradition that equals and often goes further than anything the Nazis could think up.

In denouncing the Arab-led "Zionism is Racism" campaign, America's ambassador to the world body, Daniel Patrick Moynihan, warned that, "The United Nations is about to make antisemitism international law…. A great evil has been loosed upon the world." That through political pressure the great evil of Resolution 3379 was revoked in 1991 with a one-sentence Resolution 46/86 hardly changes the matter. As a result of an incessant drumbeat of Islamic propaganda and bribery, the Jew and Israel have become identical concepts of evil.

It does not go too far to say that with Islam's organized attempt to delegitimize Israel—and Jewry itself—worldwide antisemitism would hardly be where it is today.

(e) **The American formula.** Like everything else in the world's least homogenous society, it's complicated.

Take one part each of (a), (b), and (c) above, mix gently, bake at various temperatures for at least a hundred years, *et voilà*, the toxic result is nothing less than what is probably the most multifaceted Jew-hatred ever cooked up.

The contributions of Jews have been intrinsic to America's foundation and growth. From Haym Solomon, who in the eighteenth century actually bankrolled the American Revolution; to its defense by such individuals as Uriah Phillips Levy, who in the nineteenth century rose from eleven-year-old cabin boy to commodore, at the time the highest rank in the US Navy; to the critical twentieth-century work of Rear Admiral Hyman Rickover, father of America's fleet of nuclear submarines. But these are just individuals. Consider the numbers.

In the Civil War, ten thousand Jews fought on both sides, or 6.67 percent of the Jewish population. Of America's non-Jewish population, only 2 percent were in uniform. When the US entered World War II in 1941, 5.2 million Jews were citizens of the US out of a total population of 136.7 million, making up 3.8 percent of all Americans. In the best of expectations, Jewish combatants in World War II would have reflected their percentage of the population. In point of fact, over half a million served in the military, 10.6 percent or three times their proportion of the general population.

So here's my question: Given the historical record of Jewish Americans' willingness to put their lives on the line for their country, to say nothing of American Jewry's outsized contribution to every aspect of American society from its economy to politics to law to science and the arts, why precisely did President

Franklin D. Roosevelt choose *not* to bomb the railroad tracks leading to Auschwitz or, indeed, Auschwitz itself? No single act would have better reflected recognition of America's debt to its Jewish citizens.

But it did not happen. Just as it is said Nero fiddled while Rome burned, the great hero of American Jewry, whose name was whispered in awe around the dining table of nearly every Jewish family, fiddle-faddled while six million Jews burned.

Ostensibly this was because the War Department (Newspeak had not yet been invented so as to bring forth the Department of Defense) ruled repeatedly that neutralizing the killing factories would divert resources from bombing the enemy, and that Auschwitz was beyond the range of US bombers. This is pure baloney: In many cases, the gas chambers were seconds in flying time from other strategic targets. In one instance, on August 20, 1944, a squadron of 127 US bombers, accompanied by fighters flown by the African-American unit known as the Tuskegee Airmen, struck oil factories less than five miles from the gas chambers. In fact, Allied bombers targeted the oil installations that were part of the Auschwitz camp at least twenty times, each time ignoring the ovens whose smoke rose in the sky to engulf them. At least one of those runs was flown by a twenty-one-year-old pilot who would become Sen. George McGovern, whose B-24 Liberator was ordered to target the oil fields.

"There is no question we should have attempted…to go after Auschwitz," McGovern said decades later. "There was a pretty good chance we could have blasted those rail lines off the face of the earth, which would have interrupted the flow of people to those death chambers, and we had a pretty good chance of knocking out those gas ovens." Aside from confusing gas chambers with the ovens used to burn the corpses, McGovern was right.

That FDR chose to leave this in the hands of the War Department is, in and of itself, an indefensible cop-out. It was simply not a White House priority to save Jews, part and parcel of a long string of antisemitic actions by an iconic president beloved by Jewish Americans.

The most infamous of these was America's refusal in 1939 to accept Jewish refugees from Nazism aboard the MS *St. Louis*, which had sailed from Hamburg to Havana carrying nine hundred desperate Jews. The US State Department pressured Cuba to deny them shelter, and when the *St. Louis* attempted to disembark her passengers in Florida, the state forbade their entry. Canada did the same. Eventually the *St. Louis* returned to Europe, where 254 of the original 900 were murdered by the Nazis.

Visas were, however, available for Jews who could contribute to the war effort (and even to American culture, such as writers and film directors), but not to just plain Jews who were, by definition, undesirable. When a plan was put forward in 1938 to rescue twenty thousand German Jewish children on the model of Britain's *Kindertransport*, both the president and his wife Eleanor, who made a point of her liberal values, remained silent. They let others speak for them, and there were millions, prominent among them Laura Delano Houghteling, FDR's cousin and wife of his immigration commissioner, whose antisemitism was as public as it was casual: "Twenty thousand charming children would all too soon grow into twenty thousand ugly adults." She meant us.

Those same ugly adults made up that wildly disproportionate ratio of Jews in the armed forces. These included such future American assets as three World War II medal of honor recipients—it is thought more would have been included were it not for rampant antisemitism in the military—to say nothing of a long line of legendary commanders.

American antisemitism is as complex as it is pervasive. Early on, the US considered itself a Christian nation, so a population with too many infidels was thought to be undesirable both on the grounds of religious belief (the French model) and racial stain (the German model). The English model held its own as well, because American society (in both iterations: society in general and so-called "society") rejected Jews as culturally alien, as they did blacks, Asians, Irish, Italians, Mexicans, and others whose names began or ended with alien vowels or such "Jewish" suffixes as -*witz, -berg, -man,* and *-stein.*

Even battlefield commanders who benefited from white-bread *goyish* names took precautions.

Which may explain why Mark Clark, in his time the youngest four-star general in the US Army, conqueror of Rome after leading US forces from the beach at Anzio, had himself baptized after his appointment to West Point. A decorated hero in both World War II and Korea, he carried the name of his father, a Clark, and so was able to duck the heritage of his Jewish mother, born Rebecca Ezekkiels, daughter of refugees from Romania.

A variation on this theme was to occur in the next generation with the story of another General Clark, the unrelated Wesley Kanne Clark, whose Jewish father (Kanne being a transliteration of Cohen) died when he was four. His Christian mom subsequently married the *goy* who raised him, even managing to get himself on Clark's birth certificate. Young Wesley discovered his Jewish ancestry when he was stationed in England on his way to a distinguished career that culminated with his appointment as Supreme Allied Commander of NATO. After his retirement, Clark liked to say he was descended from a long line of rabbis.

While in uniform, many Jews by birth were widely known to be careful of this kind of admission.

As a young World War II battlefield correspondent for the Jewish Telegraphic Agency, novelist Meyer Levin was assigned to scout around the European theater to write profiles of Jewish war heroes. He turned up Gen. Maurice Rose, known as one of the "fightingest" divisional commanders on the staff of General George Patton, one of the fightingest American generals ever. Born a Jew, Rose became a convert to Christianity during WWI. Levin approached the general's aide, saying, "Hi, I'm Meyer Levin of the Jewish Telegraphic Agency. I want to write a profile of the general, stressing the Jewish angle." Back came word that the general wanted no such profile; he didn't want his Jewish background mentioned. As an editorial in the *New York Sun* put it, "He had enough troubles."

Levin kept searching until he heard about a dashing young tank commander called Creighton Abrams. He finally caught up with the future general in the field. The correspondent climbed aboard the officer's tank and the colonel himself emerged. "Sir," the writer said, "I'm Meyer Levin of the Jewish Telegraphic Agency. I want to write a profile of you, stressing the Jewish angle." Abrams looked at him a bit quizzically but, without pausing a second, said, "Well, hop in."

If this sounds like the story of a proud Jewish officer— Abrams would later become Chief of Staff—no such luck: Abrams was of Scottish origin.

Considering that Jewish participation in its defense preceded even the idea of an American state by over a hundred years, when Asser Levy, a Vilna-born Jewish refugee from Brazil, demanded and won the right to be included in the guards who defended New Amsterdam, the US remains a nation with a Jewish problem, not least because it pretends to be an open society.

Ivy League colleges were long known to have quotas on the numbers of Jewish admissions, and some—though the name on the library may be that of a Jewish donor—still do. But most of us rarely have to look that far.

More than one golf club in the Hamptons, where I live, counts no Jewish members, though Jews make up a significant percentage of the summer population. Jews may be guests of members, however. Yay. Earlier on, we lived just across the street from one such beautifully tended course. When he learned that he would not be welcome, my then teenage son Ross got himself a golf club and, with a friend, played the course regularly from the ninth hole on—during the week, when the links were less crowded.

Rather more resourceful Jewish golfers would hardly have been satisfied with that when, despite their wealth, they were denied entry to Shinnecock Hills Golf Club, frequent home to the US Open, which wasn't "open" at all. So, they founded a club of their own, the Atlantic, exclusive in another way: Prospective members pay an initiation fee that could buy a nice house in one of America's most prestigious neighborhoods. This is an old story: California's once iconic Hollywood Park racetrack was founded in 1938 by Jack and Harry Warner and the equivalent of a whole *shul* full of Jewish producers, stars, and agents who were not welcome as members at Santa Anita.

Even so uniquely a Jewish institution as the galaxy of summer-resort hotels in the Catskill Mountains, a short drive from New York City, had its origin in rampant antisemitism. These hotels were "exclusive" in the original sense of the word: No Jews allowed. My father loved to tell the story of a Jewish couple named Smith—it happens—who for their wedding night reserved the honeymoon suite at a luxe hostelry several hours' drive from their home in the Bronx.

The desk clerk takes one look at them and somehow can't locate the reservation.

As politely as possible, the bridegroom asks, "Do you mind telling me what is your religion, sir?"

The desk clerk answers, "Why, I'm Christian."

"So you must know how come Jesus was born in a barn," the Jew says. "Because an antisemitic son of a bitch like you wouldn't let his parents into the hotel!"

Cultural antisemitism is hardly limited to the elite. As late as 2000, I learned that I was a "Jewboy" at a convention of newspaper publishers; it is true I was the only Jew, but many decades from being a boy. Still, a somewhat tipsy female news executive from Indiana let me and a couple of dozen others in attendance in on this little secret. I should not have been shocked. Two decades earlier, a boyhood friend, who was to become a distinguished professor of psychology, left Dickinson College in Pennsylvania after his freshman year because he was repeatedly accused of being simultaneously a "clannish" Jew and trying to pass as a Christian. He transferred to Brooklyn College, which at the time was chock full of Jews. There, Roth was not a four-letter word.

Clannish of course brings to mind the Ku Klux Klan, both in the time of Reconstruction on through the Jim Crow era and today, in its rather less formidable but still hateful twenty-first century renaissance. Now making its appearance outside the South via the same white backlash that elected our forty-fifth president, it has for the most part put aside (for now) its attacks on blacks, who tend to fight back, and altogether dropped its interest in exposing the horrors of "Papism" and Catholics, who are now well integrated into America's Christian majority.

The updated Klan was on display in the 2017 Unite the Right riot in Charlottesville, Virginia, where armed rednecks from all over the US shouted antisemitic slogans as they clashed with counterdemonstrators in a mass demonstration of the virulence of fascist nativism. The violence wrought by an estimated five to six hundred armed nazis, many flaunting swastika insignia, brought about two horrific outcomes: (a) the murder of thirty-two-year-old Heather Heyer, a counterdemonstrator who was one of a crowd rammed by a car driven by a nazi, and (b) the encouragement of more of the same by President Donald J. Trump, who dog-whistled approval of the violence by what may well be a significant representative of his voter base, saying, "You also had some very fine people on both sides." Ever since, he's been alternately defending the truth of this statement and denying he ever said it.

Meanwhile, a relatively new player has taken a seat at the Jew-hatred table, the country's growing—and increasingly vocal—Muslim community. Let us here make a distinction between the Jew-hatred of the Arab world and that manifested by American Muslims. Once thought to have put aside racial violence upon swearing the oath of allegiance, Islamic Americans have a long history of being overrepresented on the domestic terrorism front. Among the gold-medal winners in the category of *American* Islamist-inspired bloodshed:

> **1968**: In an auspicious debut of Arabs on the terrorism stage, Palestinian-American Sirhan Sirhan pioneers ideological terror in the US by assassinating presidential candidate Robert F. Kennedy. Five years after the killing of President John F. Kennedy in Dallas, the shooting of his younger brother in broad daylight at a Los Angeles electoral rally establishes murder as second only to oil as a significant export from the Arab world.

> **1990**: El Sayyid Nosair, an Egyptian-born US citizen, murders Rabbi Meir Kahane, founder in 1968 of the Jewish Defense League, whose motto, *Never Again*, outlived the JDL itself. Originally formed to protect Jews who lived in or on the fringes of black neighborhoods, the group staged audacious acts to pressure the USSR to permit

Russian Jews to emigrate. While mainstream Jewish organizations marched and demonstrated non-violently, the JDL showed its muscle at an Aeroflot office, the residence of a Soviet diplomat, and at visiting Russian cultural ensembles in the US. After Kahane's ascendance to Israel in 1971, the JDL in America slowly disintegrated, while in Jerusalem its founder won a place in the Knesset. Spurned as a racist by the political establishment of the Jewish State, his murder was quietly celebrated by those who feared Kahane's growing political power, a unique instance of mutuality between Israel and its enemies.*

2002: The owner of a small limousine service, a legal immigrant from Egypt named Hesham Mohamed Hadayet, chooses the Fourth of July to open fire at the El Al ticket counter at Los Angeles International Airport. Two people are killed and five injured, including the Israeli security guard who brings him down. Initially, authorities are confused as to whether Hadayet should be charged

---

* In the Knesset, its membership regularly walked out of the plenum en masse when Kahane rose to speak. Among his ultra-nationalist offenses was a plan, baldly stated, to complete the Jewish-Muslim exchange of population, begun with the forced exile of over three-quarters of a million Jews who had lived for centuries in the Arab Middle East. Meir's proposal was the reciprocal exile of Israeli Arabs.

When I published the Israeli daily *The Nation* in the late 1980s, I had a taste of Kahane's Treatment by the Israeli establishment when I broke the ban on giving the nationalist firebrand a chance to appear in print in editorial dialogue with a member of the left-wing Labor Party. For my sin, I was unceremoniously drummed out of the Israel Newspaper Publishers Council. To this day, stickers appear on Israeli walls that read *Kahane Tzadak*—Kahane Was Right.

with a hate crime or with terrorism—yes, you read this right—as if these are not two different names for the same thing.

2005: A group of four American-born Muslims, two of whom had converted to Islam in prison, are charged with conspiracy to attack military bases, synagogues and an Israeli consulate in California. The incident throws light on the continuing menace of US penitentiaries as a breeding ground for Islamist terror. Start with people who are already violent, add a theological and ideological rationale for more of the same, and the inevitable result will be worse than the sum of its parts.

2006: US citizen Naveed Haq, son of Pakistani immigrants, murders one woman and wounds five others in an attack on the Jewish Federation of Greater Seattle. At his trial, he blames bad medical care and mental illness. "I am not a man filled with hate," Haq tells the court. "That Naveed Haq at the Federation that July day was not the real Naveed Haq." Phew, for a moment there, we thought he was just another Islamist terrorist. Must have been someone else, according to eye-witness testimony, railing against Jews as he opened fire. Though not quite in the same league, Haq's crime was overshadowed in the press by drunk actor Mel Gibson's verbal attack the same week on Jews in the film industry. Sorry, Mel: There's a difference between actual shooting and shooting your mouth off. Maybe next time.

2009: US Army Major Nidal Hasan, a psychiatrist no less, shoots to death thirteen unarmed soldiers and wounds at least thirty others at Fort Hood, Texas. Citing a "defense of others" defense, Hasan tells the court he slaughtered his fellow soldiers in order to protect the leadership of the Taliban and what he called the Islamic Emirate of Afghanistan. This came as news to the Pentagon, which had earlier described the murders as "an incident of work-place violence." Yes, and 9/11 was just a case of some Arabs unhappy with airline food.

2011: In the thirteenth plot against the city thwarted since the Twin Towers went down— not that anyone is counting, this works out to an average of one major attack a year in New York alone—police in Manhattan uncover a plot by two Muslim-Americans to attack a synagogue and a church, and for good measure blow up the Empire State Building, this last an eerie echo of 9/11. Arrested were twenty-six-year-old Ahmed Ferhani and twenty-year-old Mohamed Mamdouh. According to the New York Police Department, their plot was motivated "primarily by hatred of infidels and antisemitism." In a sting operation, Ferhani tells an undercover officer he planned to enter the synagogue disguised as a worshipper, then leave a bomb. A police source says Ferhani and Mamdouh represent a new kind of threat: "They weren't waiting for guidance from bin Laden, they weren't looking to go overseas. They were confident they could do it themselves… They weren't driven by religion. It's really more politics and antisemitism."

2013: In the worst terrorist attack on US soil since 9/11, Chechen brothers Tamerlan, twenty-six, and Dzhokhar Tsarnaev, nineteen, set off two pressure-cooker bombs packed with nails near the finish line of the Boston Marathon, killing three people and wounding 264, among these seventeen who lost limbs. Later the brothers shot a Massachusetts Institute of Technology police officer. The elder brother is killed in a shootout with police; the younger receives a death sentence. Investigators suggested the Tsarnaevs, legal immigrants, held extreme Islamist beliefs but were not connected to a foreign terrorist group. Said to be "self-radicalized," they learned how to build explosives on the internet. Tamerlan is later implicated in an earlier unsolved triple murder. Two Muslim friends of Dzhokhar are subsequently found guilty of obstructing justice in getting rid of evidence tying him to the mass murder. A third is killed in an exchange of fire with federal agents.

2015: A married couple, Syed Rizwan Farook and Tashfeen Malik, slaughter fourteen and seriously injure twenty-three others in a mass shooting of California government workers at a Christmas party in San Bernardino. Farook is a U.S.-born citizen of Pakistani descent; his wife a Pakistani green-card holder. According to the FBI, the two were "homegrown violent extremists" who had become radicalized by "consuming poison on the internet."

2015: Mohammod Youssuf Abdulazeez, a twenty-four-year-old Jordanian immigrant who as a child became a naturalized American, opens fire at two military installations in Chattanooga, Tennessee, killing four Marines and a Navy sailor. A former high school wrestler, Abdulazeez maintained a blog in which he wrote: "Don't be fooled by your desires, this life is short and bitter and the opportunity to submit to Allah may pass you by." According to the FBI, the shootings were "motivated by foreign terrorist organization propaganda." Abdulazeez made a half dozen trips to the Arab mideast. His computer held downloaded videos by Anwar al-Awlaki, principal English-language recruiter for Al-Qaeda. See below.

2016: Omar Mateen, twenty-nine, cuts down forty-nine people and wounds fifty-three others at a gay nightclub in Orlando, Florida. In a call to police during his three-hour occupation of the premises, Mateen swears allegiance to Bakr al-Baghdadi, self-styled emir of the Islamic State. Until the infamous Las Vegas massacre the following year, it was the deadliest mass killing by a single shooter.

2016: Three bombs explode in the New York metropolitan area and several unexploded devices are discovered. Thirty-one people are wounded. Following a shoot-out with police, Ahmad Khan Rahimi of Elizabeth, New Jersey is captured. He is sentenced to life imprisonment without parole. Officials declare he is not part of a terrorist group, but his actions were influenced by "the extreme Islamic ideology espoused by Al-Qaeda" on the internet. According to NPR, a restaurant in Elizabeth, New Jersey owned by members of Rahimi's family, was "Yelp-bombed" in retaliation. That'll teach 'em.

2016: In St. Cloud, Minnesota, twenty-two-year-old Somali-American Dahir Adan is shot dead after wounding ten people with steak knives at a shopping mall. Adan came to the US at the age of two as a refugee, ultimately becoming a citizen. Reportedly he asked his victims if they were Muslims before shouting "Allahu Akbar!" and slashing away with a knife in either hand. A spokesman for the local Somali community said the attacker had no record of violence and was a good student more interested in sports than religion. Oh. Must be something he ate.

2016: At Ohio State University, a Somali refugee named Abdul Razak Ali Artan is shot dead by police after injuring thirteen, some rammed by his car and others stabbed. He is described as having been inspired by ISIS internet propagandist Anwar al-Awlaki, an American citizen assassinated via drone strike in Yemen by the US military in 2011.

2017: Mowing down his victims in a rented truck, twenty-nine-year-old Sayfullo Habibullaevich Saipov, who had immigrated from Uzbekistan seven years earlier, kills eight people and injures eleven others on a bike path in New York City. A flag and a document swearing allegiance to the ISIS are found in the truck.

2019: Mohammed Saeed Alshamrani, a Saudi Air Force officer undergoing flight training at Naval Air Station Pensacola in Florida, takes the lives of three American military personnel and wounds eight others. Subsequently, twenty-one Saudi military trainees are pulled out of the training program, apparently on the wild supposition that there may be a better idea than inviting armed Saudis to a US military base.

Maybe someone in the press or government should have connected these dots, not least of which is one dot big enough to hold the graves of the 2,977 innocent civilians murdered on September 11th, 2001, to say nothing of the premature deaths of uncounted police and firefighters who suffered medical damage from the toxic site as they attempted to rescue survivors. In all, Saudis accounted for fifteen of the nineteen al-Qaeda terrorists found directly responsible for the suicide attacks at the World Trade Center in New York, the Pentagon, and the hijacking crash of a passenger plane in Western Pennsylvania en route to another target in the capital. Regardless of origin, all the terrorists named above were either American citizens of Muslim extraction or Muslims here legally.

Hundreds of other incidents are on the record, to say nothing of many more that are not because they have gone unreported. Added up, American citizens of Muslim background and those who had entered the country legally are as of this writing responsible for the death of thousands of innocent victims and the wounding of thousands more. I would add it up, but presumably from the time of writing and the moment months later this book is, dear reader, in your hands, the numbers will rise.

But Islamist violence is only part of the problem: Americans of the Islamic faith have been increasingly *politically* active in the past decade. Guess what: They don't like Jews. The 116th Congress now has three Muslim members in the main representing districts with high concentrations of Islamic-Americans. Just as Jewish immigrants settled in areas where there were already Jews—and synagogues—Islamic immigrants (as well as Christians from Muslim countries) have been drawn to areas where their co-religionists have settled and built houses of worship. Thus, Michigan has large populations of Arab-Americans; similarly, Minneapolis has a heavy concentration of Somalis.

To one extent or another, each of the individuals representing these districts has strong views on Israel—all were in the forefront of Congressional opposition to the US moving its embassy from Tel Aviv to Jerusalem, something American presidents have promised for decades but, until Trump, never managed. These members of Congress have followed the pan-Islamic political line of equating American and other diaspora Jews with Israel itself. According to this logic, Muslims are not only at war with Israel but also with "the Jews."

This is of course hardly an American phenomenon. The 2008 attack by Pakistani terrorists on twelve sites in Mumbai, India included on its target list the city's Chabad House. Six hostages were killed, including the Jewish center's American-born rabbi and his pregnant wife. Their two-year-old son survived thanks to the quick thinking of his Christian nanny and the assistance of a Muslim cook. According to Indian government reports, the Islamist terrorists had been instructed that one Jewish life is worth fifty times the value of any other.

It gets worse. The same vicious antisemitism has come to motivate many left-wing Americans, including those in Congress. To be progressive in America today is to identify oneself not only with opposition to the existence of the State of Israel, with corresponding support for anti-Israel and anti-US terrorism worldwide, but to take on the kind of religious and cultural antisemitism that can best be described as nazism "lite." Thus, Congresswoman Ilhan Omar's calculated tweet regarding Jews that "It's all about the benjamins baby" does double duty: Not only do Jews care only about money, but because the term is heavily used among blacks, this is a dog-whistle attempt to draw Afro-Americans into the circle of Jew-hatred.*

(f) **The Afro-American style**. Arguably, many American blacks are already there. Despite the Jewish origins of the NAACP; despite the many Jews who marched for civil rights in the sixties and suffered the consequences of beatings, jail, and even death; and despite even something so fundamental to black life in America as its religious modeling on the Hebrew Bible—most Negro spirituals are based on the fight for freedom from slavery of the ancient Israelites—African-Americans tended to believe that Jews were their oppressors, especially because in the northern ghettos these were the only white faces—as shop-owners and landlords—they knew.

Though Arab, Indian, Pakistani, Korean, and other immigrant shop-owners long ago replaced an earlier generation of Jews as ghetto grocers and retail merchants, Jews remain major players in real estate in such mainly black neighborhoods as New York's Harlem and Bedford-Stuyvesant in Brooklyn.

Notable among these is President Trump's Jewish son-in-law, Jared Kushner, the highest profile landlord of black residential properties in America. According to Maryland financial disclosure reports for 2017 and 2018, Kushner and wife Ivanka have ownership stakes in thousands of low-income and government-assisted residential rental units in no less than two hundred parcels in Maryland that have been cited and fined, according to a spokesman for Baltimore County, for "livability issues such as mold, insect infestations, mice, rats, window or door leaks, inadequate air conditioning or heat, etc." Other govern-

---

* Though the use of *benjamins,* from Benjamin Franklin's portrait on the one-hundred-dollar bill, appeared earlier, in the late 1990s it became popular among African-Americans after rapper Puff Daddy released a single called "It's All About the Benjamins," followed by versions by Lil' Kim, the LOX, and The Notorious B.I.G.

ment reports bring that "etc." into dramatic focus: "Infestations of rats, mice, bugs, fleas, bed bugs, gnats, maggots, vermin or roaches." That the couple who are perhaps the best-known Jews in America are contenders for the title of slumlords of the century, with some 17,500 apartments in New Jersey, Pennsylvania, Maryland, and New York, does little to change the commonly held image among blacks that Jews are the enemy.

Are we? Not hardly. Black anger against Jews, who are seen as the face of capitalist greed, conveniently leaves out the inconvenient records of American Jews as defenders and promoters of racial justice. But it is enough to tip the scales sufficiently so that so-called progressives have managed to identify Jews with racial injustice in parallel with the identification of Israel as an apartheid nation.

To say nothing of a rewriting of history in which Jews have been cited by the same progressives as key figures in the slave trade while the Arab hand in the African slave trade has been conveniently ignored, as has been the role of native Africans like the King of Dahomey, whom historians identify as the go-to African for the slaves he kept in a warehouse ready for the next visiting slave ship.

It is a taboo fact that the sale of slaves to Muslim countries far exceeded the Atlantic trade, not least because it began in the seventh century, if not earlier. Among other researchers, Tidiane N'Diaye, a Franco-Senegalese anthropologist, puts the number of slaves exported to the Arab world at between fifteen and seventeen million. This is around double the numbers for the Atlantic slave trade, which between the sixteenth and nineteenth centuries is estimated to have totaled between nine and eleven million.

Where then are the descendants of black slaves in the Arab world? According to N'Diaye, there were precious few: "When slaves reached their destination most of the males were castrated in 'specialized workshops'." According to Professor Abdulazizi Lodhi of the University of Uppsala in Sweden, "When it came to exports, tribal Africans themselves were the main actors. In many African societies there were no prisons, so people who were captured were sold." In his monograph *Some Aspects of the Arab Slave Trade From the Sudan, 7th-19th Century*, African slavery scholar Yusuf Fadl Hasan, a Sudanese, writes, "It was for (the) military function that the Muslim rulers, especially those of Egypt and North Africa…tapped the inexhaustible traditional source of black Africans." Lest American blacks call this a Jewish invention to deflect blame for our purported dominance of the transatlantic slave trade, Hasan's study is published by the University of Khartoum, hardly a Jewish source.

Regardless of the work of Muslim and African scholars, regardless in fact of history itself, and regardless of anything but left-wing politics at its most deeply nonsensical, Afro-American antisemitism—and its concomitant alliance with so called Progressive politics—remains a farce to be reckoned with.

As are all the others.

Elie Wiesel had it right when he noted in an interview following his receipt of the Nobel Peace Prize in 1986: "There is a coalition of antisemitism today, the extreme left, the extreme right, and in the middle the huge corpus of Islam. I'm worried, I go around, you know, with a very heavy heart." Why? According to Canadian parliamentarian and Jewish leader Irwin Cotler: "The Holocaust did not begin with guns; it began with words."

CHAPTER 4

———————— ✡ ————————

Modes of Growth

Organizations, factions, and theologies based on hate must either grow or lose the momentum that excites their participants, who may then fall away out of frustration. While it is true that even the most emaciated of belief groups may hold on for a long time, the longer they exist as shadows of their former selves, the less they are a threat. This is not a hard and fast rule, not least because many hate groups change their names while retaining their characteristics, even over centuries: The hashish-fueled Assassins were the suicide bombers of their day, infecting Iran beginning in the year 1080 before moving on to Iraq, Syria, and what today is Lebanon. Suffused with hashish in this world and promised a paradise of seventy-eight virgins in the next, the Assassins were the lunatic forebears of the Islamist terrorists of our time, motivated by the same adolescent incentives.

In the history of antisemitism, violence has ebbed and flowed in erratic patterns whose only constant is its transmigration in one form or another around the world. Where it is out of fashion in one place (or where its Jews have been exiled or wiped out), it is for sure likely to arise elsewhere (an elsewhere whose Jews have not yet been exiled or wiped out).

Though anti-Jewish violence has erupted independently in many places, antisemitism began to coalesce in modern form in medieval Europe and the Middle East with the spread of literacy brought about by printing, so that by the thirteenth and fourteenth centuries, hatred and suspicion of Jews had become a standard of belief. In the Christian world, canon law, whether promulgated by local bishops or the pope in Rome, was passed down through the church hierarchy in the form of printed decrees to be read out during mass. When in recent decades a number of popes apologized for the Roman Catholic record of incitement against the very existence of Jews, they had a lot to apologize for.

Antisemitism, as we know, would not exist without an efficient medium of communication. Though the effect of Johannes Gutenberg's invention of moveable type on Jewish life (and death) was inordinately negative, from an antisemitic perspective it was merely a good start.

By the 1920s and particularly the '30s, a new medium arose which magnified rather than replaced the written word. Radio became a prime tool of Jew-hatred, followed rather lamely by television (whose licensed airwaves are more strictly controlled) and now by the internet, which combines words, pictures, and sounds in a medium that can be as viciously instantaneous as it is difficult to patrol, or even monitor.

In America, when radio preachers like Father Charles Coughlin of Detroit railed against "the Jews," his efforts were abetted and amplified by such hate-sheets as Henry Ford's *Dearborn Independent*, which on May 22, 1920 led off with a front-page article titled "The International Jew, the World's

Foremost Problem," and continued in the same vein in ninety-one subsequent weekly editions. Consistently spewing hatred and fear of Jews, the paper's front-page motto was "Chronicler of the Neglected Truth," a clarion call to paranoid xenophobia. Ford also made available to an enormous public an English translation of *The Protocols of the Elders of Zion*, the infamous Russian forgery detailing Jewry's drive for global domination. Hardly a local paper, Ford had seven hundred thousand weekly copies sent unsolicited to libraries and schools across America.

Tragically, the effect of the auto baron's madness was not limited to the United States. In book form, a multi-volume collection of material from Henry Ford's rag was widely disseminated in multiple languages around the world. It was especially well received in Germany.

With a framed photo of Ford on the wall behind him, Hitler told a *Detroit News* reporter in 1931, two years before he became German chancellor, "I regard Henry Ford as my inspiration." According to Thomas Weber's *Becoming Hitler: The Making of a Nazi*, "Henry Ford is important for having provided to Hitler confirmation, coming from the very heart of America, of an idea that had been brewing in his mind…. The idea was that Jews' control of global finance was behind the world's problems…. Henry Ford thus turned into an antisemitic icon for Hitler." Which is why Ford is the only American named in *Mein Kampf.*

One leading Nazi, Baldur von Schirach, the *Reichsjugendführer* (Hitler Youth leader) in the 1930s, claimed he became an antisemite after reading *The International Jew* in German. After the war, von Schirach testified to Ford's very special responsibility for the death of millions when he spoke at the Nuremberg trials. Before being found guilty of crimes against humanity for helping to send thousands of Viennese Jews to their deaths, for which he was sentenced to twenty years in Spandau prison, the equivalent of a slap on the wrist, von Schirach is quoted in Neil Baldwin's *Henry Ford and the Jews: The Mass Production of Hate*: "If Henry Ford said that Jews were to blame, why, naturally we believed him…. You have no idea what a great influence this book had on the thinking of German youth."

So much for your virtue-trumpeting passive-aggressive Uncle Max, who drives a Ford because he would never so much as consider a Volkswagen.

The confluent use of antisemitic radio broadcasts and Ford's widely read weekly became a model for the Nazi seizure and control of all forms of information in the Third Reich.

To that end, Propaganda Minister Joseph Goebbels had millions of cheap radios produced and distributed—just as the Volkswagen was the people's car, the *Volksempfänger* was the people's radio, cheap because heavily subsidized; by 1941, 65 percent of German households had one. And with it came Hitler's voice, reinforced by the Nazi Party's total control of publishing—newspapers, magazines, and books—to say nothing of film.

It is fair to say Goebbels would have salivated at the ubiquity of the World Wide Web today. As of 2018, accessible to 84 percent of American households, the internet's uniquely exponential efficiency in disseminating fake news (the phrase originated with the Nazis—*lugenpresse*: "lying press") would have been, and is, a propagandist's dream.

Envisioned as the morally peerless instrument of a neutral soap box open to all, the web has turned into a cesspool of lies and innuendo that the Reich propaganda Ministry would have seized on with alacrity, or maybe just seized.

Today the internet is in fact the single greatest recruiting tool of nazism worldwide. Just as vegans, feminists, nudists, child molesters, coin collectors, libertarians, and devotees of the 1972 boattail Buick Riviera have discovered strength in numbers via the internet, so too have antisemites, along with haters of gays, transsexuals, blacks, Asians, atheists, illegal immigrants, and environmentalists. Simply put, the internet has a unique ability to bring together and thus validate otherwise isolated individuals who hold passionate opinions so they are able to share and propagate those opinions without limit.

This is not the top-down preaching of radio and television. It is the masses (or as a high-school English teacher of mine liked to put it, *them asses*) coming together as an agglutinized force for evil.

But unlike the original Nazis, probably the best-branded political organization ever, such web-based hate groups as the National Policy Institute, the Charles Martel Society (its website is The Occidental Observer), the Pioneer Fund, The Daily Stormer (as in, not so subtly, storm troopers), The League of the South, The Council of Conservative Citizens, Identity Evropa, The Patriot Front, and Stormfront tend to shape-shift, changing their names when convenient. They are really not membership organizations as we have come to understand the term. They are simply dog-whistle signalers, often changing their names to evade the notice of law enforcement. According to an article by Emma Grey Ellis in *Wired,* "Two major groups involved in the original (2017 Charlottesville) rally no longer exist: the organizers, Vanguard America and the Traditionalist Workers Party." The aficionados of these and other here-today/gone-tomorrow web-based groups really don't go away but simply attach themselves to the websites of other groups, or to the same groups with altered names.

Assessing actual alt-right numbers is less science than guesswork. Stormfront may claim three hundred thousand registered members, but founder Don Black himself admits only a small fraction are active on its website, with some 95 percent of the site's visitors anonymous outsiders. The Anti-Defamation League has identified some ten thousand white supremacists on websites and on social media like Facebook. However, most white supremacists do not belong to organized (and thus easily identifiable) hate groups, but rather participate in the white supremacist movement as unaffiliated individuals, lurking on the sidelines while absorbing the message. Thus, the size of the white supremacist movement is considerably greater than just the membership rolls of commonly known hate groups.

Based on a broad set of keywords and keyword combinations put together by the Anti-Defamation League to capture hate speech, between August 2015 and July 2016, Twitter logged some 2.6 million tweets containing antisemitic language. These tweets had an estimated reach of about ten billion impressions, with the attendant effect of normalizing, reinforcing, and legitimizing antisemitic ideology on a massive scale.

Those tuning in to the ideology may be paranoid, but many are aware that they do have enemies. Many remain unaffiliated for good reason.

According to *Wired*, "Many posts about DC's Unite the Right rally call it a 'lawsuit trap.' Remember, there was a civil rights suit brought against the organizers of Unite the Right, and the judge has issued an opinion that the organizers had conspired to violate the civil rights of Charlottesville citizens, a conspiracy that could legally be tied to the death of Heather Heyer." *Wired* quotes Richard Schragger, who specializes in Constitutional and local government law at the University of Virginia School of Law: "If I were the folks thinking about participating, I could be quite worried that my participation could link me to violent activity that violates civil rights…. Even if you're exercising your First Amendment rights, you're responsible for the outcomes."

The result is that many nazis are putting aside the swastika—at least temporarily. According to *Wired*, Jason Kessler, one of the organizers of the Charlottesville rally:

…has banned the swastikas and the other symbols of white supremacy that so many objected to at the last rally. Kessler is trying to massage the movement into something (somewhat) more palatable, similar to the surviving organizations Identity Evropa and Patriot Front. Identity Evropa claims to protect cultural heritage, Patriot Front claims their prejudice is patriotism, and Kessler claims to be a civil rights advocate for white people. All of which are lies that tell the truth: the open racism we all saw at Charlottesville is being slowly pushed underground.

This has the dual effect of making nazis *qua* nazis less visible and goes a long way to explaining a curious phenomenon noted by the FBI and other law enforcement agencies: As a group, the bombers and assassins implicated in acts of racial terror over the past decade have not been card-carrying members of racist groups but simply fellow-travelers. When they step out into the light of day, these are often called lone-wolf killers, but in point of fact they are more like solo rabid wolves, infected by the virus of Jew-hatred but not necessarily running with the pack. This makes solitary terrorists difficult to identify and even more difficult to track *before* they act. Unlike an earlier generation of European Jew-haters, Nazi with a capital N and so obviously (and rather garishly) dressed to kill, potential mass murderers like Dylann Roof, convicted of killing nine people in a black church in South Carolina in 2015, are essentially fuses waiting to be lit. In the words of a manifesto attributed to the then twenty-two-year-old, Roof was frustrated by the alt-right movement's *disavowal* of violence: "We have no skinheads, no real KKK, no one doing anything but talking on the Internet…. Well, someone has to have the bravery to take it to the real world, and I guess that has to be me."

Considering that the alt-right targets Muslims in much the same way it targets Jews, it is a precious irony that regarding Jews, radical Islamists are in effect partners with white supremacists, however different the underlying ideologies.

However, as we have seen, in terms of mayhem, Islamist haters have been beating the b'jesus (b'mohammed?) out of their white-nationalist competition. The difference seems to be that Muslim nazis hate America as much as they hate Jews, while white nazis concentrate on hating—and killing—Jews.

Though Arab terrorism in America is rarely talked about, for fear that telling the truth will bring a charge of Islamophobia and thus racism, it is a fact that even aside from 9/11, Islamist violence is the camel in the American tent.

That trail of bloodshed is as long as it is out of proportion to the estimated 1.1 percent of Muslims in the US, plus a smaller number who entered the US legally. Not for nothing do otherwise innocent individualsnamed Salim and Ahmed have a problem on Transportation Security Administration lines at American and international airports: Increasingly, bad actors tend to have Arab names. Fittingly, Bobby Kennedy assassin Sirhan Sirhan had two of them.

In 1968, prehistoric times in terms of digital communication, that particular villain acted without the encouragement and assistance of Jew-hatred on the internet. It is no accident that the rise in antisemitic violence has coincided with the invention of the greatest means of communication ever invented.

Though Arab-American groups regularly disavow violence and condemn hate crimes, a Pew Research survey in 2011 found that 1 percent of US Muslims believe that in defense of Islam violence against civilian targets is "often justified" and 7 percent say such attacks are "sometimes justified." Considering that nearly 3.5 million Muslims reside in the US, this means that some three hundred thousand American Muslims believe that killing infidels is often or sometimes just the ticket. How many more of those surveyed were unwilling to admit to the same is not known, though it is a fact of life in polling that many people prefer not to admit an affinity for kiddie porn or a willingness to walk out of a shop when the cashier has made a five-dollar error in their favor.

Pew's projection that by 2050, America's Muslim population is likely to double suggests that, all things awful being equal, the US can look forward to six hundred thousand Muslims in its midst who approve of jihadist violence, not least because it is drummed into them online. Worse, we can look forward to a compounding factor: If Pew is correct in predicting that 10 percent of Europe will be Muslim by 2050, European Community passport holders can be expected to add to the threat because they may enter the US freely on tourist, student, and professional visas.

As if these numbers are not sufficiently jaw-dropping, a look at the potential for violence by white nationalists and black Jew-haters is hardly reassuring. Polling has shown that fully a quarter of non-Muslim Americans admit to being antisemites, a far larger pool of potential Jew-killers. This population has brought forth increasing numbers of swastikas painted on Jewish institutions, street violence against Jews, and what may possibly be the beginning of a copycat trend of Jewish-home invasions. As I write this, a Hannuka celebration in the Orthodox enclave of Monsey, New York was interrupted by a thirty-seven-year-old black man who broke into a rabbi's home and is being charged with the rabbi's murder and the attempted murder of four others. This followed only days after the shooting attack by two Afro-Americans on a kosher grocery in Jersey City, leaving three dead.

As well, 2018 and 2019 were banner years for white nationalists attacking synagogues in broad daylight, with eleven Jews killed at the Tree of Life temple in Pittsburgh and one at the

Chabad synagogue in Poway, California. In both cases, the shooters were denizens of the internet.

Jews in the US no longer can afford themselves the aspirational luxury of believing "It can't happen here," but must come to terms with the evolving reality that "It is happening here"—first online, then on your street.

At the end of the day, does it matter which beast intends to devour more Jews? Though our tactical response to each threat may be different, in essence we must recognize this new fact of Jewish life—and death. Because it is happening here, we must organize the counterattack.

CHAPTER 5

---✡---

Offense, the Best Defense

To do so, American Jews must come to terms with the uncomfortable idea that we must ourselves take on the responsibility for preserving American Jewish life, to say nothing of Jewish lives. But this will mean overturning centuries of Jewish passivity in the face of violence. Remember the joke about Jerry and Bob? Here's the companion piece:

Two Jews are lined up against the wall before a firing squad. When the officer in charge asks if they have a last wish before dying, one of the Jews asks for a cigarette.

Immediately the second Jew whispers, "Shhh, don't make trouble."

If this sounds familiar to anyone with a Jewish grandmother, that's because avoiding trouble by shutting up and taking it has been a hallmark strategy of Jewish survival as a precarious minority for generations. All but codified, the technique is as old as the earliest pages of Jewish history. We have only to look at Genesis 32 and 33, which tells the story of Jacob's reaction when his brother Esau, who is understandably angry that Jacob stole his birthright, appears on the horizon at the head of four hundred armed men. Rather than attempt to combat the threat with a force of his own, Jacob develops a three-pronged strategy: (1) Disperse his clan so that should one part be wiped out, another will survive; (2) Offer gifts—in this case a good deal of livestock, the cash of the day—in an attempt to buy off his hot-headed brother; and (3) Pray.

With minor excisions to keep the narrative flowing,* here is the story:

Chapter 32

7 The angels returned to Jacob, saying, "We came to your brother, to Esau, and he is also coming toward you, and four hundred men are with him."

8 Jacob became very frightened and was distressed; so he divided the people who were with him and the flocks and the cattle and the camels into two camps.

9 And he said, "If Esau comes to one camp and strikes it down, the remaining camp will escape."

10 And Jacob said, "O God of my father Abraham and God of my father Isaac, the Lord,

---

* "Goodness! Do I really have to read this, this, this *scripture*?" Alas, yes. I absolutely do not apologize for including these long passages from the Torah or, as those who have never even glanced at it, call it, the Bible. There are even some Jews who call it the Old Testament. For the latter two groups, kindly step out of your twenty-first century shell. Cheez, 10 percent of American Jews know nothing of the twenty-first century, and the rest know nothing of any other.

Who said to me, 'Return to your land and to your birthplace, and I will do good to you.'

12 Now deliver me from the hand of my brother, from the hand of Esau, for I am afraid of him, lest he come and strike me, (and strike) a mother with children.

14 So he lodged there on that night, and he took from what came into his hand a gift for his brother Esau:

15 Two hundred she goats and twenty he goats, two hundred ewes and twenty rams,

16 Thirty nursing camels with their young, forty cows and ten bulls, twenty she donkeys and ten he donkeys.

17 And he gave into the hands of his servants each herd individually, and he said to his servants, "Pass on ahead of me and make a space between one herd and another herd."

18 And he commanded the first one, saying, "When my brother Esau meets you, and asks you, saying, 'To whom do you belong, and where are you going, and for whom are these before you?'

19 You shall say, '(I belong) to your servant Jacob; it is a gift sent to my master, to Esau, and behold, he himself is behind us.'"

20 And he commanded also the second one, also the third one, also all those who followed the herds, saying, "In this manner shall you speak to Esau when you meet him.

21 And you shall say, 'Also, behold, your servant Jacob is behind us.'" For he said, "I will appease his anger with the gift that is going before me, and afterwards I will see his face, perhaps he will favor me."

Chapter 33

1 Jacob lifted his eyes and saw, and behold, Esau was coming, and with him were four hundred men; so he divided the children with Leah and with Rachel and with the two maidservants.

2 And he placed the maidservants and their children first and Leah and her children after, and Rachel and her Joseph last.

3 And he went ahead of them and prostrated himself to the ground seven times, until he came close to his brother.

4 And Esau ran toward him and embraced him, and he fell on his neck and kissed him, and they wept.

5 And he lifted his eyes and saw the women and the children, and he said, "Who are these to you?" And he said, "The children with whom God has favored your servant."

6 And the maidservants and their children drew near and prostrated themselves.

7 And Leah and her children drew near and prostrated themselves, and after (them), Joseph and Rachel drew near and prostrated themselves.

8 And he said, "What is to you (the purpose of) all this camp that I have met?" And he said, "To find favor in my master's eyes."

9 But Esau said, "I have plenty, my brother; let what you have remain yours."

10 Thereupon Jacob said, "Please no! If indeed I have found favor in your eyes, then you shall take my gift from my hand, because I have seen your face, which is like seeing the face of an angel, and you have accepted me.

11 Now take my gift, which has been brought to you, for God has favored me (with it), and

(because) I have everything." He prevailed upon him, and he took (it).

18 And Jacob came safely (to) the city of Shechem, which is in the land of Canaan, when he came from Padan Aram, and he encamped before the city.

19 And he bought the part of the field where he had pitched his tent from the sons of Hamor, the father of Shechem, for a hundred kesitas.

Well, it worked with Esau, but apparently, he was just a miffed brother and not a militant nazi.

In essence, this triad of tactics foretells the strategy for survival of diaspora Jews to this day. And both with regard to dealing with Esau and as the overarching blueprint for Jacob's descendants, it has worked. It is how we survived millennia as hated outcasts in other people's countries. If in Christian theology the Wandering Jew is forced to be homeless for the sin of rejecting Christ, the Jewish view of perpetual homelessness is far more pragmatic. The Jewish diaspora is a diverse investment portfolio in which some places are better, some worse: By putting our eggs into many baskets, some eggs will always survive to hatch another generation of chicks. If the universe remains intent on playing a game of whack-a-mole with the Jews, the Jews will keep popping up elsewhere. In the case of Jewish history, Andrew Carnegie was off the mark in 1885 when he wrote: "'Don't put all your eggs in one basket' is all wrong. I tell you, 'Put all your eggs in one basket—and watch that basket.'"

As to offering gifts, Jews have been paying bribes to rulers over the centuries for the simple right of residence. In Muslim lands, this has traditionally been in the form of a head tax paid for the privilege of living as a *dhimmi*, a second-class citizen protected by Islamic religious law (except of course when that law broke down and Jewish blood flowed in the streets). In Christian

Europe, Jews for centuries have been lending money to kings, dukes, and earls in exchange for the right of residence, though it seems to have been an unwritten rule that kings, dukes, and earls eventually rescinded that right, booting the Jews out rather than repay the loan (but not before Jewish blood flowed in the streets).

In our time, individual Jews attempted to buy their way out of Nazi-occupied Europe by trading cash, watches, diamonds, or anything of value for their lives. Sometimes it worked, but in the main, such bribes offered only a temporary solution, often only of days or even hours. Holding all the levers of power, Europe's Nazis, from the governmental level down to the lowest rung of the Gestapo and the local police, had little interest in taking bribes when they could simply take: Museums and private art collections the world over are well-stocked with paintings and other valuables that were simply stolen from Jews—and more such treasures are discovered every year.

Bribes tend to work best when the giving and taking of same are the most efficient solution. For the Nazis, there was no reason to give up the *quid* when the *quo* was there for the taking.

Perhaps the most pathetic of Jewish attempts to make a deal where they had no bargaining power came about when Nazis entered Jewish towns and villages. In my father's home village of Bhotke (also spelled Botchki), Poland, when the SS swept in, the rabbi came out with the traditional welcoming offer of bread and salt, the gesture symbolizing a willingness to accommodate the conqueror. On that day in Bhotke, the SS officer in charge simply shot the rabbi in the head, after which the Jewish population was herded into the synagogue to await transport to Auschwitz. Only a single individual of the several hundred Jews of Bhotke survived to tell the story, one which was repeated in countless villages across central and eastern Europe.

As to prayer, one of Jacob's three tactics to ward off the worst, alas, the Holocaust speaks for itself.

What speaks louder, or should to American Jews, is the very next chapter in Genesis, in which we are offered the tale of Dinah and her brothers. The contrast with the preceding chapters is so clear it is emphatic.

Chapter 34

1 Dinah, the daughter of Leah, whom she had borne to Jacob, went out to look about among the daughters of the land.

2 And Shechem the son of Hamor, the Hivvite, the prince of the land, saw her, and he took her, lay with her, and violated her.

3 And his soul cleaved to Dinah the daughter of Jacob; he loved the girl and spoke to the girl's heart.

4 And Shechem spoke to his father Hamor saying, "Take this girl for me as a wife."

5 Jacob had heard that he had defiled his daughter Dinah, but his sons were with his livestock in the field, and Jacob kept silent until they came (home).

6 And Hamor, the father of Shechem, went out to Jacob to speak with him.

7And Jacob's sons had come from the field when they heard, and the men were grieved, and they burned fiercely, because he had committed a scandalous act in Israel, to lie with a daughter of Jacob, and such ought not to be done.

8 And Hamor spoke with them, saying, "My son Shechem his soul has a liking for your daughter. Please give her to him for a wife.

9 And intermarry with us; you shall give us your daughters, and you shall take our daughters for yourselves.

10 And you shall dwell with us, and the land shall be before you; remain, do business there and settle there."

11 And Shechem said to her father and to her brothers, "May I find favor in your eyes. Whatever you tell me I will give.

12 Impose upon me a large marriage settlement and gifts, and I will give as (much as) you ask of me, but give me the girl for a wife."

13 Thereupon, Jacob's sons answered Shechem and his father Hamor with cunning, and they spoke, because (after all) he had defiled their sister Dinah.

14 And they said to them, "We cannot do this thing, to give our sister to a man who has a foreskin, for that is a disgrace to us.

15 But with this, however, we will consent to you, if you will be like us, that every male will be circumcised.

16 Then we will give you our daughters, and we will take your daughters for ourselves, and we will dwell with you and become one people.

17 But if you do not listen to us to be circumcised, we will take our daughter and go."

18 Their words pleased Hamor and Shechem, the son of Hamor.

19 And the young man did not delay to do the thing because he desired Jacob's daughter, and he was the most honored in all his father's household.

20 And Hamor and his son Shechem came to the gate of their city, and they spoke to the people of their city, saying,

21 "These men are peaceful with us, and they will dwell in the land and do business there, and the land behold it is spacious enough for them.

We will take their daughters for ourselves as wives, and we will give them our daughters.

22 However, (only) with this (condition) will the men consent to dwell with us, to become one people, by every male among us being circumcised, just as they are circumcised.

23 Then shall not their cattle, their property, and all their beasts be ours? But let us consent to them, and they will dwell with us."

24 And all those coming out of the gate of his city listened to Hamor and his son Shechem, and every male, all who went out of the gate of his city, became circumcised.

25 Now it came to pass on the third day, when they were in pain, that Jacob's two sons, Simeon and Levi, Dinah's brothers, each took his sword, and they came upon the city with confidence, and they slew every male.

26 And Hamor and his son Shechem they slew with the edge of the sword, and they took Dinah out of Shechem's house and left.

27 Jacob's sons came upon the slain and plundered the city that had defiled their sister.

28 Their flocks and their cattle and their donkeys, and whatever was in the city and whatever was in the field they took.

29 And all their wealth and all their infants and their wives they captured and plundered, and all that was in the house.

30 Thereupon, Jacob said to Simeon and to Levi, "You have troubled me, to discredit me among the inhabitants of the land, among the Canaanites and among the Perizzites, and I am few in number, and they will gather against me, and I and my household will be destroyed."

31 And they said, "Shall he make our sister
like a harlot?"

Cool, huh? Jacob is scared of the consequences (as the story continues, there are none, not least because all the Hivvites were wiped out), but his sons don't give a camel's eyelash for the consequences, if any. The Torah doesn't necessarily take the side of Jacob's sword-wielding offspring, but simply offers two choices for dealing with those who would do us ill, or in the case of Shechem, have already done it. Notice that in both cases, Jacob's clan is a minority in the land, actually just arrived, so the parallel with our time—it would seem since time began—holds true. To paraphrase what the Talmud tells us, though perhaps in more elegant terms: When a Jew-hating bastard comes to kill you, shoot him in the friggin' head.

Yeah, but with what?

According to a report based on a 2001 survey by the American Jewish Committee (now calling itself the AJC—hiding something, are we?), while 41 percent of American households possess firearms, the parallel number for American Jewish households is only 13 percent. And I may not be alone in suspecting this particular AJC survey is flawed. Outside of Texas, where I have family who, believe you me, have guns aplenty, I know quite a few American Jews and can think of only a handful of gun-owners among them, and one of those is me. No matter what the number, it is too low.

At Tree of Life Synagogue on that fatal Shabbat in 2018, none of the worshippers was armed. Had one, two, or ten members of the congregation been packing, many if not all of the lives lost would no doubt have been saved. That was precisely the scenario in 2019 at West Freeway Church in a suburb of Fort Worth, Texas when a shooter burst in, managing to fatally shoot two worshippers before a pair of armed Christians cut him down. When a machete-waving madman broke into a Hannuka celebration in 2019 in Monsey, New York, killing one and wounding four, would the bloodshed have been limited or even prevented had someone in the house been armed? Certainly there is a fair chance the answer is no. And a similar chance the answer is yes.

Still, armed Jews are not wizards capable of magically taking out an attacker (or attackers; stay tuned: assaults by *groups* may well be next year's news). Luck and circumstance will always play a part. In the Jersey City incident, where two persons began shooting with high-powered rifles from outside the kosher grocery, it's unlikely that someone inside the shop firing a handgun might have been able to repulse the attackers. Despite what the movies have conditioned us to believe, hitting a moving target with a pistol at a distance of more than thirty feet is not easy, and less so when he is shooting back. On the other hand, return fire might have stopped the attack and sent the villains to attempt escape. Or a lucky shot might have disabled one of the terrorists sufficiently so that the other might lose his or her momentum. Or an armed person on the street might have had the opportunity to shoot the attackers from behind.

Or not. But one situation in which being an armed Jew might not be effective in bringing down the assassin hardly negates all the other scenarios in which that armed Jew might very well make a difference. Alas, inventing hypothetical armed Jews is not going to arm Jews. The problem is further complicated by the fact that, despite the views of antisemites, not all Jews are alike. Among the orthodox, especially among *haredim*, whose eighteenth century eastern European haberdashery clearly identifies them as a low-hanging fruit for Jew-haters, there are problems with packing Hebrew heat. Especially on the Sabbath, when touching anything classified as a tool, even a pencil, much less a Glock 19, is an abomination. Still, the overarching teaching is that "He who saves a life saves a world." And despite Judaism's rigid rules on what Jews may or may not eat, should a Jew have to choose between a ham sandwich and death, rabbinic authorities have and will continue to opt for the ham sandwich—hell, even ham and cheese together. Even for those dogmatically opposed to firearms, in a life and death situation, the gun is that *traif* sandwich. Which is why I'm betting *haredim* might be the first Jewish cohort to arm themselves, not least because the Ultra-Orthodox tend to flock together under the absolute rule of hereditary rabbis. In this kind of autocratic society, once the head of the community rules that gun ownership is necessary, every household will have a gun, and under every long silk *capota,* a Colt.

But by most estimates, Orthodox Jewry makes up only a tenth of the US Jewish population. As for the other nine-tenths, despite firearms being inanimate objects, the majority of Jews seem as an article of faith to believe that guns, not people, kill people. In national elections, Jews tend to vote Democratic, and the Democratic Party is the party of gun control. But gun control need not be seen as co-terminus with no guns at all. We control driver's licenses, as well as licenses to practice medicine, sell houses, regulate the zoning of real estate, and even cut hair; despite controls, all of these activities continue to exist. The National Rifle Association may see any restriction on gun ownership, such as registration, waiting periods, and the forbidding of firearms to people with mental problems, as the beginning of a slippery slope to gun seizure; but this need not be the case. Voting Democratic and owning a gun should not be mutually exclusive. I know plenty of liberal gun-owners who are *goyim.* There's no reason Jewish liberals should not join their ranks.

Getting Jews to do so is another story. Outside of the *haredi* communities, Jews have no pope, no cardinals, no bishops—even pulpit rabbis have no authority when it comes to making decisions for their congregations beyond the liturgical. There's a huge difference between deciding whether the congregation should stand during the recitation of *Kaddish* and whether its members should pack heat. Convincing American Jews to emulate the tough-guy attitudes of their blue-collar grandparents and great-grandparents is not going to be easy. When three Jewish accountants walk down the street, nobody crosses over to the other side. Jewish lawyers and dentists may engender fear, but their implements of choice are not fists and baseball bats. Like it or not (and I suspect Jewish Americans do—after all, great-grandpa didn't vacation in Aruba; in fact, he didn't vacation at all), whatever instincts for violence that have been bred into Israeli Jews, their American cousins have bred out.

A further complication: There is little question that gun ownership, particularly when the firearm is carried on a regular basis, as it should be, is life-altering. Though pistols are now constructed of plastics, magnesium, aluminum, and titanium, and may weigh less than a pound, carrying one every day changes the way people carry themselves. Whether the gun is on the hip or in the purse, it is there. It must be looked after to keep it from curious children, it must be kept clean, and, in order to be a weapon and not merely a dead weight, it must be fired regularly, even if in most cases a monthly half hour on the firing range is sufficient. In a confrontation with an attacker, no one can call a time-out to read the manual or to figure out if the safety is on or off. Conscientious practice is necessary to ensure the proper reflexive response when things go awry. As they may well do.

All told, then, getting Jews to put aside their dedication to avoid getting their hands dirty will not be easy. Deciding to become Wrong Jews will doubtless take either (a) a fatal local attack that abruptly brings the threat home, or (b) a serious public relations effort orchestrated on the national level, or (c) both.

Let's hope only (b). Otherwise, Jewish lives will remain in the grip of heavily armed Jew-haters with the element of surprise on their side on the one hand and police arriving after blood has been shed on the other. Short of that, it is difficult to conceive of American Jews browsing the aisles of gun shops for that perfect weapon without something awful prodding them into it.

Most likely, nothing will accomplish this other than more atrocities, which stand a pretty good chance of happening. It is both a happy fact of Jewish life and an extremely scary one that Jew-haters need not knock themselves out to find Jewish targets. According to a 2002 report by the American Jewish Committee—you know, that Jewish organization that prefers to call itself AJC, presumably so as not to appear, uh, too Jewish—there are 3,727 synagogues in the US, plus another 144 in Canada. According to the Jewish Community Center Association of North America, to that can be added 350 JCCs, YM-YWHAs and summer camps in the US and Canada. Leaving out all other easily identifiable Jewish organizations—local newspapers, old age homes, clubs, and schools, of which there must be well over a thousand—the total comes to 4,221 targets of easy, if not inviting, opportunity.

Now let's take a guess at how many potential nazi mass murderers exist in the US and Canada. I'm talking about total nut-jobs, the kind who collect Nazi memorabilia or those who are still upset that Jews by and large refuse to accept Allah or those who walk around mumbling about Hymie. Never heard of Hymie? Twice a candidate for the Democratic presidential nomination, civil rights leader and somehow-or-other Reverend Jesse Jackson called Jews "Hymies" and New York City "Hymietown" in remarks to a fellow black who happened to be a reporter for *The Washington Post*. As a result, Jackson's campaign collapsed, which might not be the case today. The following year, I happened to be in an elevator with Jackson in Washington's National Press building. As I stepped out at my floor, I couldn't help myself. "Regards," I said, "from Hymie."

How many wholesale assassins might there be? Since no one knows, not even the wholesale assassins themselves, I'm going to take a flying leap here and put the number at…4,221.

Which means there is one soft target for every potential mass murderer in the fifty states, not including Puerto Rico, Guam, the US Virgin Islands, the Northern Mariana Islands, and American Samoa, and for sure without taking into consideration bar mitzvahs and weddings. Of course, if there are only half the potential mass-murderers of Jews as my guesstimate, this means there are twice as many targets per nazi. In other words, if I were a crazed Jew-hater whose dying wish (let's hope) is to kill lots of kikes, infidels, or Hymies, I'd be stunned by the number of choices. Personally, I'd go for the weddings: The buffet is always mind-blowing, there's an open bar, it's possible to get lucky with a bridesmaid, and nobody knows if you're on the bride's side or the groom's. As a retired teenage wedding crasher, I speak from experience. In today's America, anyone who is even potentially serious about killing several dozen Jews in the name of White Power, Black Power, or Allah is simply going to trip over Jewish targets, except maybe in Whitefish, Montana, population 7,870.

Correction: The sixty or so Jews of Whitefish and the surrounding Flathead Valley have spent the past several years being harassed by antisemites via threatening phone calls, emails, and letters after the mother of leading white supremacist Richard Spencer got into a dispute with a Jewish real estate broker. Hell, if it can happen in a metropolis like Whitefish, the 5347th largest city in the US, it can happen anywhere. Though maybe not in Ismay, Montana's smallest city, which harbors twenty-five souls. Yet even that assumption could be optimistic: At one point, at least some Ismayites were Israelites. According to my research, a Schneider and a Raskin were born there, but went off to die somewhere else. Maybe tiny Ismay as well had an unwelcome wagon of its own.

With so many targets and an ample supply of Jew-haters with access to firearms and explosives, it's actually surprising that more Jewish blood hasn't been spilt. It might well be that the forces of evil are just taking their sweet time, or that we have not yet reached the inevitable moment when the number of incidents hasn't inspired a geometric response from copycat killers. Whether it pays to wait for this to occur is a question I'd rather not consider.

CHAPTER 6

Making Them Pay

When it comes to dealing with—and defeating—anti-Jewish violence, it might be best to distinguish between strategy and tactics. Up to now, the reaction (such as it is) from the Jewish community has been reflexively tactical, with no thought to an overall strategy. As Sun Tsu wrote about twenty-five hundred years ago in *The Art of War*, tactics without strategy is the noise before defeat.

Bad things are happening more often and with greater intensity to American Jews (to Jews everywhere, actually) than at any time since the end of World War II, when antisemitism simply went underground in a kind of hiatus from history. Though not entirely. When we speak of the Holocaust, it is normal to speak of Germany. The Poles, who did indeed suffer under Nazi occupation, were not much better. This is not the place to debate which of Germany's conquered nations takes the prize for joyous collaboration, but there are contenders. In Poland, one fiercely galling example was the murder, by their former neighbors, of

Jews on their return to their ancestral villages after surviving the camps. Here, traditional Polish antisemitism combined with plain theft, a little discussed feature of Nazism that survived its defeat: Poles who were now ensconced in former Jewish homes would have to give them up to their rightful owners. The result was a nation-wide grassroots pogrom in which your average Pole *goy* in the street finished the job the departing Germans hadn't got around to doing.

In the post-war Soviet Union, a paranoid Joseph Stalin, who as a youth had studied to be a priest, continued to make it state policy to have Jews arrested for treason, tortured, and killed. In the infamous Doctors' Plot of the early 1950s, Stalin directed that the highest level of physicians in Moscow, mostly Jews, be imprisoned for plotting to poison the Soviet leadership, not least himself. By this time, Stalin had managed to wipe out an entire generation of talented Russian Jewish poets, playwrights, and novelists, foremost among them Isaac Babel, whose classic *Red Cavalry,* detailing his life as an officer with a Cossack regiment, is among the twentieth century's greatest works of fiction in any language. Possibly worse was on the drawing board: Just before his death in 1953, Stalin authorized the construction of four massive concentration camps in Soviet Asia. It is thought he was planning a huge relocation of Russian Jews.

Though his successors repudiated the Doctors' Plot and freed its victims, in the seventies, Russia turned on the Jews once again, refusing to allow them to emigrate to Israel. Only a global campaign led by American Jews, in a rare instance of active solidarity, compelled Moscow to let our people go.

Meanwhile in the Islamic world, anti-Jewish riots were fomented by Arab governments united in their need for a scapegoat for the *Naqba,* the "Disaster" in Arabic, in which the State of Israel was established by force of arms. This led to at least eight hundred and fifty thousand Arab Jews forced from their homes, most finding shelter and immediate citizenship in Israel. That is close to double the figure of four hundred and seventy-two thousand Palestinian refugees from the newly formed Jewish state that was reported to the UN General Assembly by Ralph Bunche, its chief mediator in Palestine. It is now a surreal fact of political life that the number of Jewish refugees from Muslim countries has been ignored by the international press, the United Nations, and often even by Israeli politicians; while Arab propaganda has inflated the number of Arab refugees out of all semblance to even Arab claims at the time.*

However, in Western Europe and the Americas, after World War II, antisemitic violence appeared to be a dead issue. The nauseating reality of the Holocaust, revealed when Allied forces arrived at the death camps, was sufficient as a general rule to put a gag in the mouth of Jew-haters most everywhere. After all, the Nazis and their collaborators across Europe had in the end been defeated: Nativist antisemites in Western Europe and North America wisely kept their opinions to themselves.

For a time.

That time, which may now properly be seen as an intermission lasting some seventy years, is over. Just as global antisemitism ebbed and flowed in the thousands of years since the Jewish captivity in Egypt, it has now returned in the West with a vengeance. As the last of the survivors of the death camps have died

---

*   In 2010, the Knesset passed a law requiring compensation to be part of any peace agreement to be signed by Israel and an Arab country. For good reason: Only recently do we have a price tag for the property and valuables left behind by Jews forced to leave their ancestral homes in the Islamic world. According to an Israel government report cited by the newspaper *Israel Hayom*, that amounts to $150 billion, not adjusted for inflation: $31.3 billion worth of property in Iran; $6.7 billion in Libya; $1.4 billion in Syria; $3.3 billion in Yemen.

off, offering a unique opportunity for Holocaust deniers to peddle their claims that it never happened, a new wave of antisemitic sentiment has arisen, and with it, the targeted murder of Jews, both individually and as a group. It is hardly a coincidence that in polls in both the US and Europe, a quarter of those surveyed admitted to antisemitic opinions.

Once we recognize that antisemitism has returned to the *status quo ante*, we must also come to terms with the need for a strategy to deal with it. As in a military campaign, this must begin with a clear-eyed assessment of our assets and liabilities.

(1) The first of our assets is that we now live in a world far different from that of our grandparents. Instantly interconnected by telephone and the internet, we have the ability to know what is happening and, assuming an adequate organizational structure, to move quickly in defense and/or counterattack. Here we must note that antisemitic groups share this advantage, being able to organize via internet particularly and to create virtual organizations whose members take their cues from a central authority but act on their own. The central authority—whether nazis or Islamists—may dictate a general policy of death to Jews, but its individual members, like independent cells, carry out the killing. It is my assumption that American Jewry will ultimately have the comparative advantage in utilizing twenty-first century communications to defeat our enemies, because on a level playing field, the key to victory is skill.

(2) Our enemies are no longer nation-states but individuals and quasi-legal groups. When pogroms were directed and fomented at the national level, as they were in Russia and in the Muslim world, and as perfected by the Nazis, it was difficult, if not impossible, to defend ourselves. At best, in Europe desperate Jews were able to escape to the woods and fight as partisans. But combatting antisemitic groups, whose activities our national authorities consider to be criminal, makes for a far less asymmet-

ric situation: Basically, we now have two independent groups, Jew-haters and Jews squaring off, neither supported by government. Once again, our enemies have no structural advantage: the better equipped, more tenacious fighter will win.

(3) Being a better fighter does not necessarily mean more muscle. As we have seen through generations of war in the Middle East between Arab numbers and Israeli smarts, the advantage is to smarts, especially to the more aggressive. All other things being equal, brain power has been the eminent determinant of the outcome of war for millennia. In this regard, it gives me pleasure to offer for your consideration what may seem to be a random list of names. See if you can recognize why they should take up so much space.

> Ernst Falkbeer, Johann Loewenthal, Wilhelm Steinitz, Siegbert Tarrasch, Johannes Zukertort, Savielly Tartakower, Emanuel Lasker, Akiba Rubinstein, Aron Nimzowitsch, Gyula Breyer, Rudolf Spielmann, Richard Réti, Mikhail Botvinnik, Samuel Reshevsky, Reuben Fine, Israel Horowitz, Isaac Boleslavsky, David Bronstein, Yuri Averbakh, Miguel Najdorf, Vasily Smyslov, Lev Polugaevsky, Mikhail Tal, Efim Geller, Bobby Fischer, Mark Timanov, Viktor Korchnoi, Leonid Stein, Garry Kasparov, Judit Polgar, Peter Svidler, Teimour Radjabov, Boris Gelfand.

For those readers who do not follow chess, this is a list of international chess grandmasters who are or were, via one parent or the other, Jews (and though he denied it, both Bobby Fischer's mother and father were members of the tribe). By my count, the total is 232, though I may have missed some. But what's one or two international grandmasters when we are pointing out the significance of Jewish intelligence, the very same intelligence that antisemites believe Jews utilize in our endless striving for world domination? Alas, that hasn't yet occurred, so probably we're not that smart.

By way of contrast, here, out of a world Islamic population of 1.8 *billion* is a complete list of Muslim grandmasters:

Bassem Amin, Yasser Seirawan, Salem Saleh, Mitra Hejazipour.

So much easier to count. As to the total number of American nazi international grandmasters (and for that matter German Nazi grandmasters) that's far simpler: Zero. Close readers may wish to point out Nazi Paikidze-Barnes, but she is a Georgian-American whose first name, pronounced Na' Zee, means "gentle" in her native tongue.

It is also no accident that over two hundred Jews are winners of the Nobel Prize. These make up fully a fifth of all winners (I'll spare you the list—we need the space), while Jews make up less than 0.2 percent of the world's population. I could go on to point out Jewish leadership in business, the arts, and any other field where brainpower and creativity matter. We will not, however, attempt to divine how this has come about, nor to explain why your son is failing algebra; the first being a topic that has generated much discussion over the centuries and the second being your problem, though it might be a good idea to closely supervise his obsession with video games.

Whatever makes us smarter, we is. Which is just about how your garden-variety white supremacist would likely phrase it. Not to put too sharp a point on it, if we can't outsmart the kind of people who never even heard of the Nobel Prize, we probably deserve to be wiped off the face of this earth.

(4) Money is another significant advantage. A quarter of those on the Forbes 400 list of Americans are, wait for it, Jews. Half of the ten wealthiest Americans? Yep, that too. According to a 1916 Pew Research report, on a per family basis, Jews are the richest religious group in America, followed

by Hindus, Episcopalians, Presbyterians, atheists, and agnostics (Jehovah's Witnesses are the poorest). By any measurement, the percentage of Jews with spare cash is probably consonant with the percentage of white male country singers who wear large cowboy hats on stage. Or the number of Asian students who would be studying at Ivy League universities were it not for rigged admissions. Regarding the astounding ability of Jews to become very wealthy, it turns out the antisemites are right, though not necessarily because we connive together to keep the lowest economic classes employed at WalMart, or not employed at all. It's just our thing. *Why* is not of interest here. The fact is that Jews have done very well in what Yiddish-speaking immigrants called *die goldene medina,* the golden land.

In any war, money is at least as important as weaponry, not least because the former buys the latter and can feed an army marching on its stomach for a long time, thus ensuring victory over the long run. We need look no further than the depleted treasury of the United Kingdom during World War II before the US entered the fray. Most historians agree that Great Britain would have gone the way of France and Holland had not the Japanese bombed Pearl Harbor, forcing the US into war against the Axis Powers. That Hitler foolishly declared war on Russia certainly helped the Allies win the war, but this only underscores our point: Germany did not have the resources to fight major armies on two fronts.

Resources count. And in the coming battle against those who would bash our children's heads against brick walls, we have the goods. Given a level playing field, we Jews have the intelligence and capital to defeat the rank and file of antisemites, those who actually do the shooting and plant the bombs, most of whom live from paycheck to paycheck. Which is the real reason they hate Jews: They know that by comparison, they're just plain dumb and that their principal resource is delusional hatred.

CHAPTER 7

───────✡───────

Choosing Our Battleground

Though we do have resources, these are not infinite, and even if they were, in devising strategies to contain and defeat antisemitic violence, we must prioritize.

However nice it would be to prevent the desecration of Jewish cemeteries, floodlighting thousands of acres nationwide, installing effective fencing, and setting up cameras would cost millions. None of it is going to save one Jewish life.

Another waste is the pathetic knee-jerk attempt by institutional Jewry to send emissaries to the *goyim*, particularly to the young of the species, to explain how bad Nazism was and how Jews suffered from same. Why, Hitler killed six million Jews, many of them children just like yourselves—isn't that terrible? Maybe if these children give much of a damn about dead Jews it is, but trying to reverse centuries, if not millennia, of suspicion, fear, and hatred calls to mind the phenomenon of the exceptional

Jew: "Abe, you're not like them others at all!" Abe has now been spared condemnation as the exception that actually does prove the rule: "Abe, it's hard to think of you as a blood-sucking kike bastard at all!" All the money, time, and emotional investment dedicated to dispatching to American classrooms pleasantly geriatric Holocaust survivors—not that there are many left; pretty soon we'll have to send their grandchildren—is a failed project from the beginning. As is worrying about textbooks that tell the story of Auschwitz and Sobibor or that don't. Four lines in a world history text is as likely to make a lasting impression on adolescent minds as the horror of the slave trade, even at ten lines. Telling the story of Anne Frank has proved to be a nonstarter. If all these efforts to induce sympathy are expected to reduce antisemitism, we are really in trouble, because antisemitism is growing. And making sure every schoolbook includes the word *Auschwitz* is going to take a lot of tinkering: Unlike every other country in the world, America does not have a central ministry of education dictating the contents of textbooks and curricula. In a country undistinguished for its level of education, just getting most children to master long division is a challenge.

Which returns us to the question of efficacy.

Since violence against Jews is hardly a mass movement and, considering the torpidity of the population and the strength of our democratic structures, unlikely to be one, it is not the majority of school children who must be inoculated against antisemitic violence but a tiny minority; this tiny minority is not the kind that becomes nauseated at the thought of the Holocaust but instead is thrilled by it.

Thus, spending money on so-called outreach is a waste of effort, time, and precious resources.

What we must spend on is suppressing and removing the threat from that tiny minority who are convinced Jews must be killed. When the white supremacists in Charlottesville in 2018 chanted, "Jews will not replace us!" they did not mean Jews should somehow dissolve peacefully into the ether. They meant Jews should be killed, preferably as soon and as bloodily as possible. Getting to these people must be our goal, because these are the danger we face, not the mass of Americans for whom social antisemitism is as much a part of Christian culture as cheeseburgers, sweet sixteen parties, and Friday night football.

Put bluntly, let's not bother with those who dislike us; we need to take action against those who would kill us.

That action should in fact begin with education, but not of the *goyim*. From a young age, we must teach our children never to take shit about being Jews.

This is a lofty ambition which is immediately tripped up by the very circumstances of its existence. Think of it this way: In what world would a well-known boxer be called a "filthy Jew" by anyone not armed with a gun? Were we all well-known boxers, or karate champions, or at the very least feared as being the kind of crazy Jew who fights back, we would have fewer problems. It is our very helplessness that energizes those who would attack us.

To this end, I beg your indulgence for a personal story.

In seventh grade, I made pocket money by distributing *The New York Times*—the paper paper, not the app—to the teaching and administrative staff of Junior High School 109, a looming penitentiary-like edifice in the Brooklyn neighborhood of Brownsville, then and now the city's principal breeding ground for murder and violent crime.

Before my time, in the thirties and forties, the area was a nursery for Jewish criminals who fought their way out of poverty by living off their neighbors and later, in the form of Murder Inc., functioning as the assassination arm of the various divisions of the Mafia, in New York and nation-wide. Murder Inc. was a nice marriage of Jewish violence and Jewish savvy. Because a single killing among the Italian gangs would likely result in endless tit-for-tat blood-letting, these hard Jews sold the Mafia on the wisdom of contracting killing outside the family: You need it done, we'll do it, not you, so there's no blood vengeance.

In my day, Murder Inc. was gone—its former headquarters, catty-corner from the apartment in which I grew up, was pointed out by us kids in a peculiar mixture of pride and fear. In reality, there was enough fear to go around: The neighborhood was about equally divided between Jews who had not fled to more peaceful locations, and blacks and Puerto Ricans. The nastiness was so real it was rare for a single individual belonging to one of these groups to stroll down the wrong street at night, and often even in daylight.

Unfortunately, to get from my home to JHS 109 meant of necessity walking down the wrong streets, one of which led to a footbridge over the subway tracks of the 14th Street/Canarsie Line, which here traveled above ground and eventually arrived at the northern perimeter of Greenwich Village, and thank goodness it did; it would become my lifeline for non-Brownsville oxygen. But that would be several years later. When I was in junior high, it was all about that footbridge. For anyone else going to school and back, using the footbridge was not perilous: One traveled in a pack with one's school chums. Alas, this was not my situation. I had to be at school a good hour before anyone else to cut open the bundle of newspapers and then distribute them, some fifty or sixty copies, to the various offices and classrooms scattered throughout a large four-story building. Crossing the footbridge every morning, I was alone, and never more so than once a week when I carried cash to be picked up by a representative of the *Times*; believe me, no *New York Times* war correspondent moved more quickly through hostile territory than twelve-year-old me.

One winter morning, barely dawn, it happened.

Just as I crested the midpoint of the bridge—probably only twenty yards or so, though it seemed like miles to me—a contingent of older teenagers entered from the staircase opposite. A glance behind me told me sprinting back to the other side was not going to save me either, or protect the *New York Times'* money, which I would have to make up if I lost it: an associated group of teenagers had entered from the other staircase.

I didn't have a chance, and I knew it. The odds were fifteen to one against me at the very least—I was hardly in a position to count—and I would have had trouble were the odds even. I was all of five feet tall and pre-pubescent, those confronting me mostly full grown at sixteen and seventeen years old, and probably already out of school. Defense was out of the question: I gave up the *New York Times* money as docilely as if I were being robbed at gunpoint. The problem was, this was bound to be a regular thing. I was carrying something like seventy dollars in cash, the equivalent today of ten times that, and there was no way to avoid this exercise in highway robbery: I was compelled to carry a similar amount of cash on the same day each week. How this was known I never discovered—one of my schoolmates must have figured it out—but I knew I had a week either to give up the job or figure out a solution.

Worse, I could hardly count on others for help. I'd have had to round up twenty or thirty friends to accompany me to school an hour early, or get a pistol. The optometrist's son who lived across the street did a nice business in building zip-guns, but they were notorious for malfunctioning, and when they did fire had only one bullet. Besides, I was more scared of shooting myself in the nuts than I was of my assailants. If I told my parents, they would have made me quit my job—the beginning, after all, of my long career in the news business. Asking for police protection on my way to school once a week was never even a consideration: In Brownsville, one did not talk to the cops, or be seen doing so.

Though there was no sense that the boys who had ambushed me were antisemites, I couldn't avoid thinking this was a Jewish problem. They had numbers on their side, chains and knives in their pockets, and had grown up in a culture of violence. I had a well-used library card and the fear I would mess up my bar mitzvah Torah reading.

Still, I had to do something.

A week later, my heart in my throat, I climbed the staircase to the bridge and saw my assailants standing around smoking at the far end, patiently awaiting another payday. A glance back told me there was again no escape to the rear. I reached into my book bag, that day empty of books, took a Coke bottle out and smashed it behind me, then pulled out another and tossed it forward.

There is something to be said for books: I had been reading about the defenders of the Warsaw Ghetto, one of whose weapons was the Molotov cocktail. Unfortunately, I was not sure lighter fluid would explode the way gasoline had done during World War II.

It did.

The look of shock on the faces of my assailants is one that lives with me to this day, as well as the pissed-off resolve that replaced it when they realized they could step around the burning puddle. I had expected this. I pulled two water pistols out of my book bag, first spraying forward at the gang's feet, then behind me.

Their pants now aflame, they fell all over themselves trying to put the fires out. This I could not allow to happen. I marched forward with both water guns, mostly empty of lighter fluid now, pointing at them, my assailants melting back like the waters of the Red Sea.

That was it: I never had trouble on that bridge again, though for weeks after, I carried Coke bottles full of lighter fluid and those water pistols, both of which I emptied into a sewer before class. Lighter fluid reeks.

When I think back on it, I realize how mad I was: I had never tried out the process and so was betting everything on its working. But it was all I had. American Jews are not quite in that bad a situation today, except of course for the fact that like me at twelve, we are compelled to defend ourselves without recourse to allies or law enforcement. We will speak later of finding confederates, though these may be less than dependable when the chips are down. As to the police, they can't be everywhere, protecting Jewish property and Jewish lives twenty-four hours a day; anyway, their main function is not to prevent crime but to pursue criminals after the fact. After the fact is always going to be too late.

But as noted above, we do have resources, and can develop these if only we put our minds to it. And our hearts in it.

CHAPTER 8

— ✡ —

Changing the
Jewish Mindset

If you have ever wondered how the Jews survived and from time to time flourished in a diaspora with the odds stacked against us, one clue is the book in your hands. Most any book, in fact.

With no state, no army, and no dependable source of income, we Jews survived because of universal literacy, enforced by law from the first century CE for all male children (we'd have done twice as well had the ruling included girls). In the Muslim world and in Christian Europe, throughout history, Jews were the only ones who could read, write, correspond, and keep records. We were not only the people of the book, but of book-keeping. Commerce outside of simple local barter could not have existed without us. It is true that the monasteries retained Latin as a written and read language, but the monks existed in a kind of theocratic hothouse dedicated to preserving the literary and philosophical treasures of Greece and Rome so as to apply that knowledge to the developing Roman Catholic Church, and to a lesser extent, its Eastern Orthodox cousins.

Armed with Hebrew as a common written language, Jews became a kind of human Rosetta Stone, able to correspond with their co-religionists wherever in the world a denarius, obol, libra, or tetradrachm was to be made. Even today, when *haredi* Jews wish to move funds across national borders outside of regulated channels, they employ a system built not on guarantees or security deposits but, as in the Middle Ages, on mutual trust. When we sold our home in Israel, we were stuck with the resulting mountain of shekels. At the time, banks were forbidden to change local currency into dollars. I was in the States and contacted a *haredi* friend, who arranged for a second *haredi* to meet Leigh at a pre-arranged spot—with lovely irony, it was outside a bank. There, she handed a black-hatted bearded stranger a paper bag of Israeli shekels that represented most of our worldly wealth. Even more weird, she never knew his name.

Two weeks later, in New York, the dollar equivalent for the entire amount, minus a modest commission, magically appeared in our American bank account. This was a system of international banking that is two thousand years old. And it still works.

Literacy was the key to Jewish survival everywhere. In English-speaking America, our skills with language (and the sophisticated thinking that grows from those skills) have brought Jews unparalleled prominence as authors, journalists, lawyers, politicians, song writers, and film producers and directors. But American Jewry's concentration solely on English has led to mass abandonment of the national, religious, and cultural language of the Jews. Hebrew is taught and utilized in America's orthodox schools from nursery school on up, but for the vast majority of Jewish children, it is either not taught at all or so tenuously instructed that most children of bar mitzvah age are unable to read the forty or so words that comprise the blessing before the Torah. As to the Torah itself, *fuhgeddaboudit.*

American Jews are more conversant with the story of Jesus than they are with the Ten Commandments. The intellectuals among us are on more solid ground on the Reformation and the theological distinction between Shiites and Sunni than they are in naming the three forefathers and four foremothers of the Jewish people. Ask ten Jews at random outside of the Orthodox community if they have ever read the Book of Genesis and the result will almost certainly be a batting average hovering just above zero.

Why should it be otherwise? American Jews are not so much atheistic as they are apathetic regarding all things theological. In the main, our children study French, Spanish, and even Chinese, but not Hebrew in any serious way. Likewise, outside of the Orthodox, if at all, our kids are exposed to the Torah in simplified form in English, and to the Talmud not at all.

Why should this be a problem?

Because Hebrew and the basic texts of Judaism are the keys to Jewish identity, in the twenty-first century as it was in the first. In learning Hebrew from kindergarten on, American Jewish children identify as Jews. Clearly sitting down to a *seder* meal is not enough. Though according to a 2012 survey by Pew, 70 percent of Jews said they had sat down to a Passover *seder* in the past year and 53 percent said they had fasted for all or part of Yom Kippur, the figures present a more positive picture than the reality. Assuming American Jews are not significantly different from other Americans in this regard, half of our demographic is under thirty. It is our older generations who are more likely to take part in traditional Jewish ceremonies. When this older cohort dies off, what will be left?

Even so, how many of any generation can say they actually participate in Jewish ritual? On the High Holy Days, synagogues are packed with "visiting" Jews who are bored to death: Not because they have no interest in religion, but because they can't read Hebrew. Likewise, most American Passover *seders* have deteriorated to festive meals with no *Haggadot* in sight. If they are on the table, only the generation of Grandpa Sam can slowly enunciate the words before the entire charade breaks up and the food is brought out.

The fact is, American Jewry is trapped in a spiral: Little Hebrew leading to a tenuous Jewish identity, leading to no Hebrew, leading to zero Jewish identity.

Making this worse is the false concept of sole identification: No one claims that being a Christian must displace being an American, or being a Spanish speaker somehow cancels out being an English speaker. Yet American Jews are predominately sole identifiers. To be Jews somehow signifies a deletion from one's identity as an American.

Getting such sort-of Jews to care enough to fight the nazis among us is not going to be easy, though, as we've seen in the previous century, antisemites and Nazis make no distinction between self-identified Jews and those who were baptized, between those educated in Hebrew and those whose education was in German or French, or those who are the children of a Jewish mother or the descendants of just one great-grandparent.

Depressed enough? There's more.

Even for those who do identify strongly as Jews, who can read Hebrew, who celebrate Jewish milestones such as circumcision, bat and bar mitzvah, marriage, and funerary rites, the vast majority suffer from Holocaust Enchantment Disease, an influenza that has turned Jewish identity on its head since the first films of Auschwitz and Buchenwald were shown in newsreels at American movie theaters.

Instead of seeing ourselves as the joyful-to-be-alive remnant who survived the greatest genocide in history, which wiped out over half of the world's Jewish population, we have deified its victims while cutting ourselves off from identifying with them.

We see the Holocaust as a tragedy that happened to *them*, a tragedy we memorialize with tasteful monuments—challenge: name a major American city without a Holocaust Memorial—but to which we have the same relation we might feel to the Cro-Magnon, or for that matter to the once-thriving *shtetl* culture of Eastern Europe. For American Jews, as defined in the famous opening lines of L. P. Hartley's novel *The Go-Between*: "The past is a foreign country: they do things differently there." Note that Hartley didn't write: "They *did* things differently there." What he was pointing out is the ongoing existence of another world, one parallel to ours, but independent of it, a world we recognize but with which we do not identify.

Thus it is that American Jews have found themselves slammed between not knowing who we are and ignorance of whence we came, which amounts to not knowing how others see us. Alas, *we* don't see ourselves primarily as Jews, but *they* do, and a good many of *them* would rather *we* were dead.

CHAPTER 9

─────── ✡ ───────

From Generation to Generation

When a person targets an individual for violence because he or she is a Jew, that person is a nazi. It does not matter whether he is white, black, Muslim, or Martian. When you are facing someone brandishing a baseball bat, it's not the ethnicity of your attacker that is significant, but the baseball bat. This is as true for the most heinous act of violence as the most petty and common, the bullying of children in the schoolyard, say—or, if your child attends a Jewish school—on the way to and from.

Of course, children get picked on for any number of reasons: size (too short, too fat, even too tall), race (anything from Asian, Latino, Native American to black and white), religion (don't be a Roman Catholic where everyone else is Protestant, and vice versa), and even defects in speech (school can be as perilous for stutterers as for Jews) or looks (are near-sighted kids still called "four-eyes"? Probably.) Like stutterers, Jews can work hard to disguise or otherwise conceal their identity, but Jews who pass for gentiles are not our subject. Our subject is Jews who don't: Jews, that is, who are—whether proudly or uncomfortably, or both—Jews.

Schoolyard bullying is part of school life, and no matter the target, he or she is always picked on for the same reason: perceived weakness. When this perception is shared by others in the peer group, we are looking not at a one-on-one situation, but a situation of all-against-one. Thus, the most efficient way of preventing the latter is to forestall the former. A Jewish child's best defense against group violence is going on the offensive against at least one member of the group. How? By learning to fight, early and well. Antisemites of any age do not mess with the Wrong Jew, the one who is capable of inflicting pain and humiliation on his would-be assailants.

Quite clearly, this means the principal athletic activity of Jewish children ought not to be tennis but karate, not basketball or golf but *krav maga*, the hand-to-hand fighting system developed by the IDF based on the most efficient forms of pre-emptive close quarter counterattack. As it happens, *krav maga* (contact battle) was developed by Jewish wrestling and boxing champion Imi Sde-Or in the 1930s when, as Imre Lichtenfeld, he led a group of Slovak Jewish athletes against antisemitic street violence.

Krav maga training centers may now be found in most large Jewish communities; where they are absent, schools of karate, judo, aikido, kung fu, and boxing are as common as public libraries and will do fine. In other words, if you are looking to teach your children to bloody the nose of a violent antisemite of any age, you should have no trouble locating someone who can teach them just how to do it.

As we will see in other areas of learning to be the Wrong Jew, the problem is not lack of resources but of the will to employ them. Believe me, as a child of the streets in a bad neighborhood, no one wants to pick on the kid who is at least willing to inflict pain on his or her attacker.

Today's Jewish children need not resort to lighter fluid to defend themselves.

But most will not voluntarily forsake the virtual violence of computer games for the real work of learning actual violence, and most parents would rather see them on the tennis court than in the dojo. A good part of this may be laid at the feet of American Jewry's obsessive desire to see their children as upwardly mobile kids whose sport of choice is that which is most socially acceptable and which will stand them in good stead as they climb the rungs of a money-based social hierarchy. Does this mean they may not learn to ski? No, it means they may also learn to ski, but should they be on the slopes at Aspen and someone calls them a dirty Jew, a left hook is going to be more pertinent than the right schuss. To strain the language further: The greatest slalom is not going to guarantee even an imperfect shalom. Not only is teaching our kids to be the Wrong Jews going to save them a lot of pain individually, but it is going to instill in an entire generation the will to forsake the dubious pleasure of standing together holding noble placards and instead destroy those who would destroy us.

Just as we persist in teaching our children enough Hebrew to get through their bat and bar mitzvahs, so too must they learn the rudiments of self-defense as they come of age in an increasingly dangerous physical world.

To make that a standard part of Jewish education means that Jewish schools and community centers must not only offer *krav maga* and other forms of martial arts, but make these a requirement for graduation or membership. My wife has been teaching dance for decades, in the most recent of which hip-hop has edged out ballet as a child's first choice; nevertheless, those who would study hip-hop are compelled to learn ballet as well. So too, advanced calculus and a nice uppercut need not be mutually exclusive.

When on Hannuka we celebrate the victory of the Maccabees over the Hellenized Syrians, who as our political masters, aimed to destroy Jews and Judaism, we ought to remember that our enemies were not defeated by a seventy-mile-an-hour serve, but by Jewish farmers who became guerilla warriors. Despite what you were taught in kindergarten, the true miracle of Hannuka was not that a day's worth of oil lasted eight days in the newly re-consecrated Holy Temple, but that a ragtag army that had learned the rudiments of asymmetrical warfare, when the term did not exist, overcame one of the world's great armies. The miracle of Hannuka was not made by the Almighty, but by people little different from ourselves who chose to fight rather than surrender. Having earlier beaten their swords into plowshares, they learned to beat their plowshares back into swords.

We must do the same, especially when we consider that the next generation will likely bear the brunt of antisemitic violence on steroids.

Unless our children learn to defend themselves, they will grow up to be adults incapable of the same. To prevent such suicidal passivity, our kids must be exposed to rigorous training from early on, which training must continue as a lifelong pursuit. We must make sure that the physical defense of Jews as individuals and as a community remains a priority past middle school, that Jews—male and female and of all ages—become figures of fear: That those who hate us because they see us as superior add to their list of jealousies the knowledge that three Jewish accountants strolling down the street are the Wrong Jews to mess with.

CHAPTER 10

Scarier Accountants

This may be a challenge, but not an insurmountable one. Like most Americans, secular Jews pursue sports and physical activity from youth through old age—to corrupt the words of Juvenal: *mens judaeus in corpore sano*—in the belief, probably true, that in extending their muscles, they will extend their lives. Absent statistics, I suspect data on gym membership would show Jews at least as diligent in pursuing physical health as their non-Jewish neighbors, possibly more so, not least because non-Orthodox Jews tend to outdo gentiles in acting like…well, gentiles. Not to belabor the point, but German Jews were known for being more German than Germans, English Jews for pursuing Englishness, and American Jews for being more American; I'm always shocked when I fly into Houston that I'm one of the few at the airport wearing a Stetson and cowboy boots—all the "real" Texans seem to prefer baseball caps and sneakers. Since upper-middle and upper-class American culture demands the kind of lifelong interest in participatory sports (to say nothing of hours at the gym), swapping in boxing, karate, and *krav maga* for tennis, golf, and jogging should not be much of a trick. Self-defense, by which I mean the ability to achieve physical dominance over an assailant, should at least be on the menu.

But dealing with more lethal threats is quite another thing: putting adult nazis in their place calls for more than knowing how to deliver a disabling punch. At the very least, it calls for an understanding that one doesn't have to be baptized to feel comfortable in a fistfight or handling firearms, in essence that self-defense—whether personal or institutional—should not be limited to dialing 9-1-1. David did not defeat Goliath with a tennis racket.

At the end of the day, like it or not, the single determinant of who wins a war of survival will be firearms. Because once the guns come out—and they have, along with the Jewish victims to prove it—we do not wish to be, as the joke has it, the guy who brings a knife to a gunfight. Or worse, a well thought-out argument. On the streets of Queens, Marquess of Queensberry does not apply.

Why then is it that when it comes to guns, American Jews are such wusses? The answer is both social and cultural.

The first has to do with the tight bundling of liberal ideas in the traditional platform of the Democratic Party: one person, one vote; freedom of expression no matter how offensive; a woman's absolute right over what happens in her own body; regulation and even prohibition of gun ownership. Though the numbers have eroded a bit over time, Jews still support the Democratic Party over the Republican Party by more than three-to-one—probably because their parents did and because Jews associate liberal values with the protection of minorities. Though this may change as the generation of baby boomers dies off, 70 percent of American Jews say they are Democrats or lean toward the Democratic Party, while 22 percent are or lean Republican. Among Orthodox Jews, the balance tilts in the other direction: 57 percent are or lean Republican, and 36 percent are Democrats or lean that way. But remember: Only 10 percent of Jews identify as Orthodox.

Will Jews ultimately abandon the Democratic Party, the party of the less well-heeled? Maybe not.

Outside of the Orthodox, it is difficult to find significant numbers of Jews of any age who feel comfortable with religion in public schools, limits on free speech, and laws that prohibit or severely limit abortion. In general, such people are called Republicans. Jews are in fact so adamant in their commitment to the Democratic civil rights agenda that they are as adamant for highly integrated schools as they are for sending their own kids to schools that are not.

In not quite the same way, but with parallel hypocrisy, Jews abhor guns while their own synagogues, schools, homes, and persons are increasingly subject to armed attack. In this, we are like those extreme animal rights advocates who would venture naked and unarmed into a jungle: When the rights of wild beasts to eat us are greater than our right to defend ourselves, we have entered a fantasyland where the desire for a perfect world has neutralized our ability to see the world as it is.

The world as it is *is* rather a dangerous place for Jews at the moment. And as the Argentine writer Jorge Luis Borges put it, "The world, unfortunately, is real."

Just as most of us understand that Israel cannot exist without an efficient army to defend its existence in a perpetually hostile neighborhood, and that being armed like Sparta does not preclude a co-existent civil polity that recalls Athens, so too must we unbundle from our treasure chest of liberal desires the wishful thinking that we can magically remove from the hands of our tormentors the instruments of that torment. Gun ownership by

American civilians is per capita the highest in the world, with a mind-numbing 120 firearms per one hundred citizens. Ain't nothing short of an eleventh plague going to change that. Thus, to defend ourselves against those with guns, we must embrace gun ownership for ourselves. One can advocate civil and abortion rights, freedom of speech and assembly, and any other plank in the liberal canon, and still be for the right to bear arms. In other words, it's okay to be a Democrat and pack a .357 magnum. More than okay, it is necessary. Just as it is necessary for Israel to have an army and for your kid to know how to bloody the nose of a bully at school.

Aside from its being outside the mantra of liberal values, another factor stands in the way of a sensible attitude to Jewish communal self-defense.

In essence, it is a belief system that has been part of the fabric of Jewry since our exile and dispersal from the Land of Israel: that our best hope of survival is to depend on the governments of our countries of exile; that without a state our own, without an army and police force of our own, we have no other choice. This idea is hardly refuted or even disputed by the living example of the State of Israel, but instead underscored by it: *Israelis* can do it because *they* have their own state; *We* can't because *we* don't. Compared to the organic agency of Israelis in the Jewish State, American Jews might as well be living in Poland of the 1930s or 1630 Yemen or 1430 Spain. As then, our sole agency remains limited to attempting to *affect* some small aspect of the society in which we live.

Yet despite the wet dreams of antisemites, we are far from affecting the control of much of it.

Though Jews are significantly overrepresented in Congress, we are as limited as any other minority in controlling even our immediate environment. This is not a result of antisemitism, but a feature of a vigorously fragmented representative democracy in which no minority entirely gets its way. The likewise frustrated include abortion rights advocates, evangelical Christians, gays, Catholics, blacks, small-business owners, Latinos, vegans, and nudists; in fact, any minority in a polity made up of minorities. Further, a close look at any American majority will reveal that any seeming majority is itself actually an alignment of minorities. The legislative agenda of the very Orthodox communities of Spring Valley and Monsey or Crown Heights and Long Island's Five Towns have precious little in common with the politics of secular Jews in Manhattan, only a half-hour's drive away. It is safe to say most Manhattan Jews are secular, and that they would never vote for an anti-abortion congressional candidate, but the Jews of Spring Valley and Monsey, in fundamentalist consonance with their Evangelical Christian brethren, are firmly in the anti-abortion camp. As they are with regard to gays, to say nothing of keeping federal aid flowing to religious schools—the Ultra-Orthodox may have more closeted gays among them than they are willing to admit, but all their schools are religious. To cut those schools out of federal and state aid would bankrupt the entire system of yeshivas and seminaries.

Thus, it is a mistake to believe that the Jewish vote, further fragmented by the thinning out of reliable voting precincts as Jews have migrated even unto Hawaii and Alaska, is going to have the power to do more than superficially influence national policy in either party. The same Democratic Party which bred such loyalty in American Jewry that a framed photo of Franklin Delano Roosevelt was as much a feature in Jewish homes as the little blue-and-white collection boxes of the Jewish National Fund, is now steered by progressives who would in a heartbeat erase the State of Israel and replace it with Palestine. As to the GOP, increasingly that party has lost its ideological principles and whatever moral compass it had in lining up behind a president whose heedless pandering to the great unwashed has led to such dystopian lapses as this year's presentation of press passes to a "news organization" called TruNews.

Just in case you missed it, five members of same were invited to fly on Air Force One to cover President Trump's trip to the 2020 World Economic Forum in Davis, Switzerland. What is TruNews? Look no further than its leader and founder, one Rick Wiles, a pastor no less, who the same month characterized Trump's impeachment as a coup planned by "a Jewish cabal." Several months earlier, Pastor Wiles explained it this way in a news analysis as pungent as it is poisonous: "That's the way Jews work. They are deceivers. They plot, they lie, they do whatever they have to do to accomplish their political agenda. This 'Impeach Trump' movement is a Jew coup, and the American people better wake to it really fast." Not enough? "When Jews take over a country," Wiles added, apparently for the sake of historical perspective, "they kill millions of Christians."

And all this time we thought it was the other way around.

When two members of Congress, Democrats Ted Deutch of Florida and Elaine Luria of Virginia, wrote the White House to ask why TruNews had been invited (not allowed, invited) to fly to Davos as legitimate members of the press along with representatives of Reuters, AP, and the *New York Times*, they received no reply.

But surely Jewish political power is what led the Trump administration to move our embassy from Tel Aviv to Jerusalem, and to approve Israel's annexation of the Golan Heights. Not hardly. Though these moves benefitted Israel, and are in tune with the Zionist sympathies of at least some American Jews, their real target was the Evangelical community that makes up a goodly portion of Trump's political base.

The real true news is that the political power of Jews in the United States is now about equal to the power of Jews in the United Kingdom and France. This is not quite as bad as it was in pre-World War II Poland, or in Poland at any time in the last thousand years, but it seems to be getting there.

How bad was that? Allow me to introduce you to a bit of Kestin family lore, according to which, we are descended from a former king of Poland. Quite something, right? You'd think so. Except…how does a Jew get *to be* king of Poland (or, for that matter, anywhere else)?

The story begins with a sixteenth-century Polish nobleman named Nicholas Radzivil, who seeks counsel from the Pope for the expiation of his sins. The Pope tells him to dismiss his servants and travel around Italy as a beggar. In Padua, the local rabbi takes pity on him and gives him sufficient funds to return to Poland, where the rabbi's son, Saul Wahl, is studying (by some accounts: teaching) in the yeshiva of Brisk. The prince finds the son, is suitably impressed by his intelligence, and eventually helps him become principal advisor to King Stephen Báthory. Upon King Stephen's death in 1586, the assembled Polish nobles are deadlocked on who will replace him. Awaiting the arrival of the tie-breaking vote, and aware that the throne may not be empty for more than twenty-four hours, and aware as well that a Polish king may be removed only by death, they designate Saul Wahl as king. When the tie is broken, the nobles end Saul Wahl's reign of one day with his death.

Though the tale is wreathed in legend and disputed detail, it is especially precious to my family, whose name until the turn of the twentieth century was…Padua. While it is a matter of pride to claim descent from a former king of Poland, it is also a caution. A Jew may rise to the highest seat of power in the diaspora, but it is not likely to last forever. Even in the United States, where Jews have accumulated wealth and power, we might as well be Saul Wahl, king for a day.

Unable to manifest our own destiny, as Israel's Jews do every day without a second thought, the fate of American Jewry is to vote for a candidate and a party and hope for the best. In certain places and in certain times, sometimes it works out. Mostly not.

This year, following attacks on Orthodox Jews in New York and a fatal attack in neighboring New Jersey, New York governor, Andrew Cuomo, ordered the State Police to detail troopers to guard synagogues. My own synagogue in Southampton benefitted from this protection, and just in time too: Funds had run out that week to pay the $800 a week for two armed guards during Shabbat morning services. This is hardly in the same category as the security budget of other *shuls*—the annual security budget for a major synagogue on the Upper East Side of Manhattan is said to be $650,000—but enough for our congregants to be grateful for the protection of the state.

That morning, I looked up from my prayer book to notice that the State Police car that had been parked in the driveway was no longer there. Donuts, an emergency, a call of nature? What's the difference? For some nazi staking out the synagogue for the chance to unload his AR-15, this was all the time necessary for a bloodbath. Worse, the following week, Cuomo's state troopers were nowhere to be seen. And they never returned.

The fact is, dependence on outside protection, whether private or public, is as much a guarantee of safety from marauders as prayer or a locked door. And even were armed guards stationed outside, how would they know who was getting out of his car to pray with us and who to prey upon us? As well, when our rent-a-cop's four-hour shift is done, who protects the synagogue, to say nothing of the rabbi and his family who live on the property?

No one. Unless those using the *shul* are themselves armed. Equally bad, who protects Jewish homes from attack? When the residents of a home in Monsey were targeted by a lone attacker wielding a machete, the Orthodox family celebrating there was able to fight back; but there is no fighting back when the weapon of choice is a semi-automatic pistol with ten rounds or a military-style rifle with thirty.

How soon will French-style invasions of Jewish homes come to the United States? Probably as soon as nazis figure out this is a fine way to finance their activities and at the same time torture and kill Jews. If you're not armed when they come to the door, you are out of luck: they will tie up your wife and children, possibly rape them, and then have you transfer funds offshore via your e-banking account. At that point, you will not only be useless to your assailants but a danger in that you can identify them. Besides, what nazi doesn't relish the thought of killing Jews? But if you have a gun and know how to use it, you have at least a chance of your family's walking out of the situation alive. Your children may be traumatized, but they will live to get over it.

Given these two scenarios, which would any rational individual choose? Of course, there is always the persistent hope in the kind of liberal irrationality that says not only that it can't happen here, but that it can't happen to me. If that is your thinking, please forgive me for offering in evidence the lives of some six million Jews, whose annihilation remains silent witness to your profound irresponsibility as a spouse, parent, and human being.

Or you may prefer to say, in unrelenting pursuit of fecklessness: Sorry, but my city or state does not sanction the concealed carrying of firearms, and Lord knows I am a law-abiding citizen.

Nice try, but as it happens, all fifty states permit keeping firearms at home. Even the City of New York, probably the least permissive firearms jurisdiction in America, permits the ownership of loaded long rifles and shotguns, and a twelve-gauge shotgun with an eighteen-inch barrel is not only suitable for home protection, but specifically designed for it.

Then there is another cop-out that nice Jews are likely to suggest, which brings to mind Albert Camus's classic line: "There is always a philosophy for lack of courage."

This particular lack of courage is nicely consonant with the idea of Jews as devoted, if not superior, parents: Keeping a gun in the house is inherently dangerous. What if little Shoshana or young Noah gets curious about that shiny .38 in your bedside table? Kids are curious, right?

They are. And because they are, Shoshana and Noah should not only be made aware of the danger of touching that gun, but should be with you on the range as you practice. In fact, depending on the size of the gun and the size of the child, your kids should know how to handle firearms for the noise-making fun of it and because Jewish children in the twenty-first century need to grow up as Wrong Jews, not only willing to defend themselves and their families as they grow older, but capable of same.

Though we have now put paid to the loony belief of many Jews that somehow America's nazi nightmare will melt away like an unseasonable snowfall in spring, there remains the rather more pragmatic question of how to prepare a generation to transform themselves into Wrong Jews.

Straightaway we must face reality: Though we can wait until gun ownership becomes a necessity, which is by definition too late, we can accelerate Jewish gun ownership via what is essentially a non-profit marketing campaign. To do that, it will be necessary to form a national Jewish gun-owners group, possibly under the auspices of the National Rifle Association, or far better with support from a selected number of gun manufacturers. If this tie-in sounds a bit too commercial, bear in mind that arms dealers now face a highly competitive market in which more guns are chasing fewer buyers: Opening a new market segment would be a gift for companies in the arms business, who may well be willing to support a Gun Owning Jews Organization (GOJO) via advertising on Jewish sites in times of stress for the Jewish community, which is to say advertising when antisemitic violence breaks into the news, which is to say pretty much all the time. GOJO would then be in a position to coordinate training and certification. Jews love certification. "My son the doctor" has in recent decades been expanded to "My son the doctor, lawyer, and MBA." Why not add MSS for Master Sharpshooter?

Too cynical? Perhaps, but with the possible exception of hunting, fear of victimization is already the single greatest motivator of gun ownership in the United States. Regardless of race, religion, and social class, Americans keep guns in the bedside bureau because we know the worst can happen at any time. We keep them in the glove compartment because there are crazies on the road who will ramp up road rage to murder. And we carry them where legal (also where illegal) because, uh, you never know. Gun manufacturers and firearms dealers are aware the .357 magnum they make and market will be purchased for protection. This is not a weapon for plinking, competitive target shooting, or hunting: it is meant to take out the bad guy.

Selling to Jews on the same rationale is thus not going to be exceptional, aside from the fact that up to now, Jews have not been seen as natural advocates of firearms. Yet this kind of campaign both takes advantage of Jews' legitimate fear of antisemitic violence and provides an antidote. If this is cynical, so is advertising for vitamins, cars with advanced safety features, and electronic pendants that summon help when you've fallen and can't get up. To a great extent, much of marketing is built on the idea of defense: toothpaste isn't sold only because it may prevent cavities, but to defend against bad breath, and deodorants ensure us against socially offensive body odor; the very concept of insurance—life, health, home, auto—is designed to protect us from financial catastrophe. It hardly strains the imagination to see guns in the same light: We buy insurance not because we know something bad will happen, but because it might.

The irony here is that Israel, in its monkey-see, monkey-do emulation of all that is wrong (and right) with American culture, has over the past twenty years worked diligently to limit and even prohibit private ownership of firearms. In my time in the (very) Old Country, from 1970 to 1990, I kept guns at home and very often carried, and not only because as a journalist, I was frequently in areas of what can be called demographic danger. The same 9mm Colt Combat Commander I carried during my army service, I carried concealed when I traveled in Arab areas, and even in Tel Aviv and Jerusalem. When I was not at home, my wife kept a 12-gauge shotgun handy—called by Jews and Muslims alike by the Arabic term *abu-hamsa,* the father of five (shells)—not least because we lived in the countryside within shouting distance of the old 1948 border, the Green Line, the other side of which is hugged by Arab villages controlled before 1967 by Jordan. As they do still, Israeli and non-Israeli Arabs circulated freely on either side of this conceptual borderline, which led inevitably to incidents of terrorism by a tiny minority of local Arabs. Once, when I got a surprise twenty-four-hour leave from military duty, I had my driver stop our jeep a couple of hundred feet from our home so as not to awaken Leigh and the kids in the middle of the night. As I carefully unlatched the French doors in our living room, I came face to face with the business end of our *abu-hamsa*, on the other end of which was my wife.

"Don't shoot," I said. "It's just me."

She put up the barrel. "How was I to know?"

That was early on. By the time we left Israel, the government was making it harder and harder for civilians to own personal weapons. One famous tale, possibly true, concerned an old-timer whose license to keep a pistol was not renewed because the Interior Ministry had discovered he had a criminal record. "What criminal record?" the old guy asked. He was told he'd been convicted in 1947 for illegal possession of firearms. "Yes," he said. "By the British. I was a gunsmith for the Haganah." He never got his license.

On the other hand, IDF soldiers on active duty bring their guns home with them as a matter of course, which indicates a level of readiness should the nation be attacked. With no army to protect us, US Jews have no such luck. Unarmed, we are forced to fall upon the three tactics Jacob employed when his brother Esau appeared at the head of four hundred armed men: Disperse so that a remnant may be saved, bribe, pray. It doesn't take a military genius to see that what worked for the Jewish people over centuries in the diaspora is not going to be helpful in an attack on a Jewish home, synagogue, or school. Are we really ready to sacrifice the lives of some to save the lives of others, or to attempt to negotiate a pay-off with those whose singular aim is the shedding of Jewish blood? For all of those Jews who would depend on prayer, I'm at a loss except to say there is nothing mutually exclusive about praying and returning fire.

Regarding the safety issue of guns in the home, it's a real thing. Guns must be ready at hand, in case of an existential emergency, but protected from curious children. This should not be so hard to accomplish. After all, a firearm is simply a tool designed for a specific purpose, no different in its way from a hammer that may hit one's thumb or a circular saw that might remove a limb. In every case, a bit of skill and a good deal of caution tend to forestall accidents. For that matter, while most cars are now equipped to ameliorate the effects of collision, or even to avoid same, and we all use seatbelts, no one is suggesting we give up driving because the death toll on our roads is currently thirty-nine thousand souls a year.

Though there are no statistics available indicating that more Jews are buying guns, in at least three New Jersey municipalities within a short drive from the site of the machete attack in Monsey, New York, police officials say gun permit applications jumped 50 percent after the incident. Local gun shops and firing ranges continue to see a new sort of clientele: According to the manager of a nearby firing range, "Sometimes there's so many religious people here, you'd think you're in a synagogue."

In my synagogue, at least three congregants come to pray carrying firearms, two of them with licenses, one without. At least one other member intends to apply for a pistol license, as does the rabbi. As I keep telling him, he might as well avoid the massive paperwork and the nine-month delay and simply keep a shotgun in the Holy Ark along with the Torah scrolls—unlike concealable pistols, long guns require no license. On the other hand, were I the rabbi, I'd want that handgun on me at all times: in the Hamptons, where the population is split between those in houses worth millions and the carpenters, plumbers, and handymen maintaining them, he's the only guy in a black hat and long beard, and as such, conceivably even more a target outside the synagogue than in it.

Of course, just being armed is not enough to effectively defend against predators. This became apparent when two of our armed congregants realized they were not only sitting together, which might mean they could be wiped out quickly, leaving the *shul* totally undefended; but worse, the line of fire to the door from where they sat would be straight through the women's section. Though the two have been seated together for years, it was clearly time to separate. As well, all three of those who regularly bring firearms to *shul* often practice shooting at a range of five to ten feet, pretty much the standard for bringing down an adversary indoors. But from where they sit, twenty feet is more like it. Protecting a synagogue is not quite the same as protecting one's home, or defending against an attack in a nighttime parking lot.

In addition, because we have a lot of on-again, off-again congregants, it's clear the rabbi should be reminding the assembled worshippers from the pulpit, preferably every week, to hit the floor at the first sign of an attack. Regrettably, the most common reaction in such a case is to run. In our synagogue, not only is there no place to shelter outside of a narrow doorway to the kitchen—the pile up would become an abattoir—but congregants who do not take cover in place would put themselves in danger of being shot by the very people standing to defend them.

Do-it-yourself defense is complicated. It calls for professional training and effective practice. Even the choice of weaponry should not be left to whim: some calibers are more effective at short range, and even the length of pistol barrel comes into play. A snub-nose revolver, whose barrel is two inches or less, is very effective at the normal distance of an attack within a home or on the street, yet even in the hands of seasoned shooters, is likely to be wildly inaccurate at twenty feet or more.

Guns alone are not filled with magic bullets. But without guns, we may be doomed individually to live in fear and as a community to be little more than…

CHAPTER 11

<figure>✡</figure>

Kosher Sitting Ducks

I t is a fundamental tenet of military theory to put yourself in the shoes of your adversary. Were you the enemy, what would you do? The best chess player thinks many moves ahead by anticipating the intentions and reactions of his opponent. If American Jewry is in a war with an enemy who is dedicated to our destruction, it is clear we must take steps beyond teaching our children *krav maga* and keeping a shotgun on the high shelf in the hall closet. Put plainly: What protects us from mass murder?

Too often we have seen attacks on synagogues because these are obvious targets and, by and large, undefended, easy pickings. After such attacks, Jews all over the country become aware they may be next. In the main, our reaction has been either defensive (let's get armed guards) or demonstrative (let's wave placards as we march to show we are united). The first hardly rises to the level of a tactic, while the second merely provides hate groups with an opportunity for counterdemonstrations. Not only do these do nothing to neutralize violent antisemites, but they actually encourage them by providing a venue for publicity.

Meanwhile, the success of armed attacks on Jewish physical institutions—here defined as places where Jews are likely to congregate—is likely both to encourage copycat attacks and to increase the number of potential targets, even as congregations move, however marginally, to find ways to protect their premises. Cameras have been set up, an Israeli firm is leasing red-button alarms to be installed in multiple spots in order to bring law enforcement on the double, armed guards are being hired, and in some places police forces are being detailed to post a squad car in front to discourage malefactors.

Each of these responses is glaringly imperfect.

Cameras and alarms ("I've been shot in the head and can't get up!") come into play only after an attack; armed guards stationed outside the premises are unlikely to know the difference between a Jew approaching with his *talit* in a velvet bag and a terrorist carrying a machine-pistol with a forty round clip in the same sort of velvet bag. Is it impossible for a nazi to find himself a skullcap and learn to say, "Shalom?"

In many countries, particularly in Latin America but now spreading to Europe, synagogues do not admit strangers without their having phoned in advance to answer such questions as: What is your Hebrew name? What is this week's Torah portion? Where do you normally *daven*? What is the name of your rabbi at home? Visitors to Mexico or Argentina are routinely turned away from synagogues because they fail these tests. And they do fail, not least because, ironically, secular Jews seem drawn to synagogues abroad though they would not set foot in one at home.

As a last resort, American synagogues and Jewish gathering places could emulate this level of caution, but the price is high: So many *shuls* in the US make it a point of pride to keep their doors as wide open as possible, the most significant of these affiliated with the Chabad movement, whose principal aim is evangelical. Chabad exists to draw Jews back to Jewish practice. It is a rare Chabad rabbi who would tell his congregation not to drive to *shul* on Shabbat; the whole idea of Chabad is that the smallest bit of adherence to Jewish law and tradition is far better than none at all. Conservative and Reform houses of worship keep their doors wide open for an additional reason: At a time of declining synagogue membership, an unwelcoming attitude is hardly designed to bring in new congregants to share both the pleasure of community and the cost of maintaining it.

Were American synagogues to emulate the strict security practices of synagogues abroad, not even the most stringent interviewing of newcomers is likely to be 100 percent effective in keeping out a determined terrorist. Once the questions are known, and they can be discovered immediately via a telephone interview the day before, convincing answers can be created.

How about installing magnetometers of the type used at airports, government buildings, and courthouses? Alas, they're both too invasive and insufficiently effective. Will *shul* goers agree to empty their pockets and take off their shoes to pass through a metal detector, or to stand still and raise their arms as a guard passes a portable device over their bodies? As well, such a solution assumes the non-existence of the kind of polymer pistols that can be put together on a 3D printer using specifications found on the internet and constructed with no metal at all.

Then there is the question of bombs. Think how easy it would be for someone to carry a *talit* bag or a purse stuffed with C-4 explosive into a synagogue, or a gym bag into a community center. A brick of plastique will destroy a truck. Among others, this sort of explosive is both widely available, whether stolen from US military supplies or imported from Iran, a major producer. Even a relatively shallow background in chemistry is enough to cook up an effective bomb at home. In 1995, Timothy McVeigh and Terry Nichols, two white supremacists armed with a high school education and a twenty-foot Ford truck full of fertilizer, blew up a nine-story federal building in Oklahoma City. The dead numbered 168, with 680 injured. The blast caused an estimated $652 million in damage. Of course, a *talit* bag of similar material would be far less effective, but still powerful enough to destroy a small *shul* and kill its occupants. But surely explosives monitors would detect it? Only if that detector is a dog. In which case it might be best if Fido and his handler stick around all week: letter bombs, to say nothing of anthrax-loaded FedEx parcels, may be just around the corner.

Hardened doors and windows, locked gates, armed guards, metal detectors, explosives sensors, dogs? *Dogs*? Assuming any of this works, who is going to pay for it?

CHAPTER 12

———— ✡ ————

The Economics
of Insecurity

There's an old story about the Jewish diner complaining to his waiter: "This food tastes terrible, and the portions are so small!"

In terms of the kind of security measures now being recommended for synagogues, the result is at best doubtful and the cost is astronomical. Recording digital cameras can cost $1,000 each and at maximum efficiency serve only to identify an attacker after his work is done; think multiple cameras per synagogue. Special locks retrofitted on older buildings cost the same, and are often stronger than the door's hinges, which tend to fall apart when the door is kicked in. Some security experts recommend magnetic key-cards, the kind commonly used in hotels, so that only synagogue members can enter, but these systems are not cheap and are as ineffective as any other illusion. Want instant entry into a synagogue (or hotel room)? Wait until someone with a proper key-card comes up and put a gun to his head. Magically, his secure entry is yours. Same for keypad locks with combinations. Replacing windows and doors with bulletproof glass is often recommended, a solution as silly as it is expensive: If a nazi with a high-powered rifle wants to massacre Jews, he could do worse than find a disguised ambush spot and knock out dozens as they exit the synagogue in a pack, which is the usual way we exit *shuls*, especially after the last piece of chocolate babka disappears from the *kiddush* buffet.

Which leaves us with armed guards. These come in two flavors, the kind our taxes pay for, who drive around in American-made cars with an annoying array of lights on top, or private security guards, many of whom are the same cops, retired, or active duty officers moonlighting on their day off.

Recall that incident in which New York governor Andrew Cuomo, responding to a flurry of antisemitic attacks, ordered NY State Police to guard synagogues state-wide? There is a good reason the patrol car parked outside our synagogue disappeared after the first Shabbat and never returned: If there are enough state troopers and cars to guard New York's one thousand synagogues at least one day a week and on holidays, then, fellow taxpayers, our state constabulary is seriously overstaffed and overequipped. Looked at the other way, if troopers are stationed outside of synagogues all that time, who is going to pull you over for a broken taillight?

As to local police departments, odds are they are similarly understaffed, and often there's an element of conflicted interest. In some municipalities where local cops moonlight as private guards, said local cops would be out of work if their municipalities provided the same function for free. In many places, local officers own the companies supplying off-duty cops for private work. So even if a county, town, or village is blessed with a bumper crop of cops sitting around munching donuts twenty-four hours a day, the entrepreneurial police powers that be aren't going to cut themselves out of extra income.

Depending on state and local police is thus no solution at all. Really, our cops have better things to do. At best, that is mostly about responding to a crime scene after the crime has been committed.

So, by default we are left with private guards. From the point of view of protecting synagogues, at first glance it seems not a bad idea at all.

Except it is. In fact, deploying armed guards is a terrible idea. Say a synagogue pays a private cop (or a public cop moonlighting as such) to sit in his car outside the synagogue, or even to stand by the door. Now say you are a Jew-hater with murder in your heart, a .45 in your belt, and another in a shoulder holster concealed by your jacket. How would you ever get by this armed guard?

For starters, you might simply wish him a pleasant good morning and stroll into the sanctuary, a simple enough feat since said armed guards are not about to examine male visitors for circumcision. On the other hand, after you've shot up the *shul* to your satisfaction, you may wish to be on your way. In that case, it might be a good idea to have first capped the armed guard after you wish him a pleasant good morning as you come up the steps. From your white nationalist point of view, doubtless a shame: the guard is probably not a Jew (otherwise he'd be inside praying); on the other hand, he *is* protecting *them*, which counts for something. In any case, if knocking off an armed guard is all that's keeping you from doing your part in reducing the Jewish population, why not?

To forestall such a scenario, I convinced my rabbi we ought to have an inside man as well—actually, we could really get away without Mr. Outside for all the good he would do in an actual assault, but the congregation apparently feels safer with a visible presence on the outside. This would seem to make as much sense as driving while wearing two seat belts, but in reality, the inside man, discreetly seated just inside the door, would be in a perfect position to take out the assailant from behind. Let's assume our Jew-hating assassin is aware of this, and there's no reason he wouldn't be, because he could easily have visited the synagogue earlier pretending to be just another curious Jew totally ignorant of Jewish practice. Chabad synagogues, which make up a quarter of American *shuls*, get them all the time, others somewhat less. How would you, dear reader—in your role of imagining how the enemy would act—handle *two* armed guards?

Need more time to work this out? I didn't think so. You would of course enter, knock off Mr. Inside, and then, when Mr. Outside flies through the door at the sound of gun shots, delete him as well. At this point, the synagogue and its occupants become totally defenseless, a free-fire zone.

David Pollock, now director of public policy and security at the New York Jewish Community Relations Council, whose network includes about a thousand synagogues and six hundred Jewish schools, agrees. Commenting on the 1986 terrorist attack on Istanbul's Neve Shalom synagogue, Pollock told *Ha'aretz*, "The first thing they did was take out two armed police officers. The attackers shot them with automatic weapons. Having armed guards is not a panacea."

But wait. Let's say a couple of armed guards could in some wishful way protect a synagogue and its congregants. At what cost? Someone is going to have to pay for this.

Surprise: It's you.

True, the US Department of Homeland Security in 2020 was expected to spend $90 million on its Nonprofit Security Grant Program for "target hardening enhancements." But that number is not solely dedicated to Jewish installations. The line at the public trough includes churches, schools, and community centers of all kinds. As well, New York State offers funding to yeshivas and Jewish day schools in the amount of thirty-five dollars per student, which means a school with four hundred students would be eligible for fourteen thousand dollars to cover the one-time cost of security assessments, staff training, equipment purchases, and security guards, though the last category would eat through that in a matter of months.

Worse, there is every probability that legal challenges to these disbursements will arise based on the First Amendment to the Constitution, which not only forbids the establishment of religion, but prohibits government favoring one faith over another. Considering that Jews make up only 2 percent of the US population, won't other religious groups demand their commensurate share? To say nothing of the fact that applying for grants, whether federal, state, or foundational, can be a frustrating process, and even if successful, offer a solution that is neither immediate nor particularly effective.

Even minimally, the cost of protection is staggering, especially at a time when contributions to Jewish organizations have been falling and falling.

And falling. This doesn't mean Jews are giving less to charities; they're just giving less to Jewish charities. Increasingly, those checks are being written to fund museums, symphony orchestras, ballet companies, and scientific research. A woman who survives breast cancer is liable to look at her annual ten thousand dollar contribution to some Jewish cause and abruptly decide to split this with the American Cancer Society. It is known that the very wealthy heirs of very wealthy Jews tend to include in their contributions the secular charities their parents didn't bother with: The older generation might have been content with being big fish in a Jewish pond; the younger prefers seeing their names listed as backers of a traveling Andy Warhol exhibit or a new pavilion in some municipal park. Thus, even at the same level of giving, Jewish institutions are being cut out.

At the same time, the expense of defending synagogues and other Jewish physical institutions has grown from almost nothing to numbers few of us expected ever to see, not least because few of us expected to be targets of antisemitic violence, which is supposed to have been a thing of the past. At the minimum, armed guards at synagogues alone are going to cost one hundred dollars an hour for an average of five hours a day for some sixty days a year, the minimum to protect worshippers at Shabbat and holiday services. Multiply this by the number of synagogues in the US and Canada, 4,221, and the cost is over $250 million. Every year. We can triple this amount to account for armed guards for Jewish centers, day camps, and schools, all of which require security at least ten hours a day (Jewish centers in particular are open from early morning to late at night, seven days a week), and will require more security than even the biggest synagogues. Why? Jewish centers often are made up of multiple buildings with numerous entrances, plus a lot more visitors coming and going at all hours. "A billion here and a billion there," as the late Senator Everett Dirksen put it. "Pretty soon we're talking about real money."

Unless, that is, we eschew the services of paid armed guards and take it upon ourselves to protect our synagogues, day camps, community centers, and schools. Is this possible?

It is, in the way it's possible in Israel, where every public school is protected by parents stationed at the main (and normally only) entrance to the grounds. Yes, business venues—even supermarkets—hire their own guards, a cost that is reflected in the cost Israelis pay for consumer goods, in effect a virtual tax on everything bought and sold. But when it comes to schools and synagogues, security is DIY. My synagogue in the village of Karkur never had to post an armed guard outside because so many in the congregation were carrying inside, including IDF soldiers on leave. We were our own protectors.

American Jews will have to emulate the Israeli model. But once again, we bump into a social obstacle: Too many American Jews stubbornly persist in playing ostrich, their heads in the ground and hoping for the best.

Meet Rabbi Michael Adam Latz of Shir Tikvah, a Reform congregation in Minneapolis. Apparently, it is called Song of Hope for good reason: In November 2018, only days after the fatal shooting at Tree of Life synagogue in Pittsburgh, Rabbi Latz told *Haaretz*, "We know we cannot arm our way to safety. It doesn't work. So we're going to keep our commitment to radical hospitality and keep our doors open for all the wandering and wondering who are looking for deep connection to Jewish life."

It gets worse: That Friday night, Rabbi Latz proudly announced, "The local Catholic church and an interfaith group are lining up on the sidewalk outside Shir Tikvah to welcome us to our services. Part of our building a safe community is being in deep relationships with our neighbors."

Really? What's the other part, singing "We Shall Overcome" a whole hell of a lot louder? Has the good rabbi not noticed that antisemitic violence is not likely to come from nice people just like him?

Clearly, this kind of thinking suggests American Jewry needs a national organization dedicated to the defense of Jews and their institutions, one that will provide wise guidance in making choices that are not confined to singing *Kumbaya*, plus the security expertise to implement same. Why doesn't something like this exist?

Alas, it does.

CHAPTER 13

───────── ✡ ─────────

Top Down or Bottom Up

I t is called the Secure Community Network (SCN). It was established in 2004 and funded by the Conference of Presidents of Major American Jewish Organizations, the Jewish Federations of North America, and the American Jewish Committee to provide "a coordinated approach for community wide notifications, crisis management, and security measures emphasizing common standards for enabling Jewish communities throughout North America to embrace and evidence a culture of security awareness, preparedness, and disaster response and resiliency." If you're not sure what this bureaucratic jargon means, the next sentence on the SCN website explains it, sort of: "SCN operates a full-time threat and information sharing center to monitor and report on threats and security events impacting the American Jewish community."

Still hazy?

Mainly, SCN offers pamphlets, both in print and online, along with videos, and almost all of it not merely a rehash of anodyne advice from the Office of Homeland Security, but the actual material. This is like calling 9-1-1 for an ambulance and being told to download a brochure from the American Medical Association. In short, the heavy hitters who run organized Jewry in America have attempted to solve a problem and managed instead to create a new one: "Here, look, we got this under control. So stop worrying!"

Under its previous chief, according to an article in *The Forward,* it turns out senior managers of SCN had serious conflicts of interest: Many were principals in the very same security firms they were recommending in their role as SCN employees. Following these disclosures, SCN's board brought in Michael G. Masters as its new president.

Really?

A security professional with a Harvard law degree and a master's from Cambridge, Masters has tons of experience. Not least, Masters is "of counsel" to The Soufan Group, an international security firm, and president of The Soufan Center, described on its website as a "dynamic team of research and policy analysts." Not was. *Is.* Leaving aside the question of perceived conflict of interest, Masters is clearly president of two security organizations, presumably dedicated full time to, uh, both. In terms of security for Jews, it appears to be limited to Masters himself.

If this is how America's major Jewish organizations intend to protect us from antisemitic violence, two words come to mind: *Oy* and *vei.*

Be that as it may, in January 2020, SCN took a major step forward—after sixteen years of existence—in releasing a white paper called "Firearms and the Faithful: Approaches to Armed Security in the Jewish Community." This delineates the advantages and disadvantages of institutional security via local police, armed guards, security services, and pistol-packing congregants. Ultimate recommendation: a cop or uniformed guard out in front, based on the supposition that such a presence is likely to deter an evil-doer.

Agreed. Unless said evil-doer shoots the cop in the temple on the temple doorstep, at which point he will be free to mow down Jews as casually as he would plink at tin targets at some innocuous county fair.

The white paper rightly notes that armed congregants may not be as well-trained as cops or armed guards, are less likely to be able to summon back-up police via radio, and may shoot wildly and injure innocent worshippers, in which case the synagogue may have a liability problem. Don't laugh: In 2004, a rabbi performing a circumcision was sued for medical malpractice after cutting off too much of an infant's penis. (Relax, it was surgically re-attached.) Where did the circumcision take place? Pittsburgh's Tree of Life Synagogue. Ostensibly, a *shul* that does not provide adequate security may face legal claims in case of injury or death.

This is precisely the kind of strategic thinking one can expect from the leaders of organized Jewry. We're worried about dead Jews; they're worried about lawsuits from their orphans. If so, the ideal defense in such a lawsuit would be two armed guards out front, steel-reinforced locked doors that may be opened only with a code, zero admission of strangers, bulletproof glass in all windows, and prayer shawls made of Kevlar, plus a recently discharged Marine sniper squatting in the Holy Ark.

Clearly there is no limit to spending on defensive theatrics—bomb-sniffing dogs, anti-drone technology?—but there is a limit to our ability to pay for it. As to their efficacy, we've dealt at length on how one or even two armed guards can be quickly neutralized, and key-codes may be overcome by putting a gun to the head of a congregant. As to depending on a hardened perimeter of locked and reinforced doors and bulletproof glass, Israel learned that lesson when, in 1973, Egyptian forces swept through the Bar-Lev line of bunkers on the Suez Canal in the Yom Kippur War, a tragi-comical re-enactment of France's deep faith in the quickly overrun Maginot Line in World War II.

And yes, innocent bystanders may well be cut down by friendly fire when armed congregants attempt to take down an attacker; and as well their heirs may sue the pants off the synagogue afterward. But thinking about legal problems is disturbingly academic when we're looking at life and death. After a fatal attack, what synagogue president or community center chairman will want to say that out of fear of a lawsuit, firearms had been banned on the property? Certainly, with *no* armed Jews in place, congregants stand a good chance of being mowed down by very unfriendly fire indeed. In that case, will there be anyone left to sue?

As difficult as it may be for many of us to accept, more Jews will perish unless our communities take responsibility for security upon themselves. The top-down approach that assumes we Jews cannot take care of ourselves is like asking the Pentagon for help with a rash of neighborhood burglaries, or calling the federal Centers for Disease Control when you've got a cold that won't quit.

Though the Almighty did get us out of Egypt and in the Sinai drowned Pharaoh's pursuing chariots, historically Jewish resistance to antisemitic violence has not come from above.

In 167 BCE, the Maccabees rose up against Israel's Syrian masters, who encouraged the high priest to exercise naked in public in the Greek fashion. After a guerilla war that lasted seven years, the Maccabees were victorious, a far greater Hannuka miracle than one day's oil being sufficient to light the re-consecrated Holy Temple for eight days.

From 66 to 136 CE, three popular rebellions broke out against Rome.

In the First Jewish Roman War, instigated by Rome's plunder of the Second Temple and mass executions of Jews, a popular Jewish revolt led to the massacre of some six thousand Roman legionnaires at Bet Horon. Though rebel leader Shimon Bar-Giora put together a fighting force of fifteen thousand, it was ultimately unable to overcome what must have seemed an endless supply of Roman legions. Today, when they complete their training, IDF soldiers climb to the top of Masada, where in the year 74 the last Jewish holdouts committed mass suicide rather than surrender.

In what is known as the Kitos War, 115–117 CE, revolts against Roman antisemitism broke out in the Jewish communities of Cyrenaica (present-day Libya), Cyprus, Iraq, and Egypt. Over four hundred thousand Romans were killed before Rome's legions crushed the rebels.

In 132–136 CE, Shimon Bar Kochva led a third and final rebellion against Roman rule, establishing an independent state in part of Judea for over two years. It took twelve Roman legions, as many as sixty thousand professional soldiers sent from all over the known world, to finally quell the revolt.

All of these grass-roots uprisings came about against the wishes of the Jewish authorities, whose moderation in the face of brutal treatment by *goyim* may be seen as foreshadowing the equivocation and moral surrender of America's Jewish leadership when Europe's Jews were being gassed as vermin.

While America's Jewish elite enjoyed coffee and photo ops with President Franklin Delano Roosevelt, in the forests of Europe, small groups of Jewish partisans defied hunger and freezing temperatures to attack and harry the Wehrmacht and its puppet allies. In Warsaw and other ghettos, desperate Jews rose up against the Nazis, ultimately fighting to the last man and woman with little more than pistols and Molotov cocktails.

The history of modern-day Israel reveals the same pattern: Were it not for the efforts of such groups as the Irgun and Lehi (the so-called Stern Gang), which defied the leadership of the *Yishuv* by challenging the authority of the British Mandate in Palestine, His Majesty's forces might have hung on in Palestine for decades. The leaders of the Yishuv were so doggedly determined to avoid open warfare with the British, they cooperated with the Mandate authorities by informing on the rebels.

Anyone see a pattern here?

Today, the leadership of the Conference of Presidents of Major American Jewish Organizations, the American Jewish Committee, the American Jewish Congress, and the Anti-defamation League of B'nai B'rith, in cooperation with the rabbinical organizations that claim to represent all three major strains of American Jewish religious practice (except of course the majority of American Jews who identify with none of them), issue public statements, organize demonstrations, sit down for interviews with the press, and otherwise do the minimum with the most publicity, as they have done with the Secure Community Network, an effort as well-meaning as it is toothless.

Why is this so?

As in the horrific days of the thirties and forties, when Germany ground the spirit and ultimately the life out of Europe's Jews, America's Jewish organizations are run by limousine Hebrews in bespoke suits and shoes they'd never think to shine themselves, whose idea of fighting back is, as it was then, the egregiously passive policy of "standing together." Just as the grandees of Jewry through the ages preferred cooperation with our oppressors to cutting throats and tossing bombs, the nabobs of American Jewry are reluctant to get their hands dirty.

You may have heard the definition of a Zionist as a person who hires a second person to send a third person to Israel. Now we have the parallel definition of a Jewish leader as a person who pays a second person to organize a third person to demonstrate with a sign that says *We Stand Together!*

These are the people Jews look to for leadership, a fact that would be comical if once again it does not turn out tragic, as it shows every sign of becoming.

The simple lesson of Hillel continues to echo in our time: "If I am not for myself, who will be for me?" Depending on others is a recipe for failure, whether the police, armed guards, or the clueless talking heads of the leadership of the American Jewish community, itself a made-up term that is meant to sell the idea of a single Jewish polity so that big-headed plutocrats can claim to "lead" it. The very idea that one size fits all Jews is a convenient fiction: The old joke citing two Jews, three opinions if anything underestimates the fractious nature of American Jewry, whose vitality is based in religious, political, social, class, and even geographical distinctiveness and division.

Whereas antisemites make no distinction among Jews, Jews sure do: *Haredi* Jews may appear to outsiders to share a culture, but in fact each group is so proud of its differences from the others that they make a point of minor differences in dress, social structure, and attitude from other *haredi* Jews, all of whom look down upon the so-called Modern Orthodox, beardless but devout, who themselves look down upon their Conservative and Reform brethren, but also dismiss the equally devout Chabad *hasidim*, whose synagogues account for a quarter of all Jewish houses of worship in the United States and an even higher percentage abroad, as "the religion closest to Judaism."

What the Ultra-Orthodox do have, divided as they are into sects whose leadership is inherited with a rigor the Hapsburgs might have envied, is the kind of deference to their own patriarch that makes the concept of the divine right of kings seem like parliamentary democracy. Among *haredim*, what the rabbinical leader says is law. Consequently, if that leader decides every member of the community must carry a gun, pistol-packing will become as much a part of their daily life as praying three times a day.

The Orthodox make up only 10 percent of America's Jewish population, and the Ultra-Orthodox no more than half of that. According to a 2013 report from the Pew Research Center, 18 percent of American Jews call themselves Conservative, 35 percent Reform, and 6 percent Other; while 30 percent claim no denominational identity. Moreover, those who publicly identify as Reform and Conservative are known to be only tangentially what they claim to be. Beyond an outsize craving for bagels and lox, most are best described as Jews who would visit a Reform or Conservative synagogue if they visited a synagogue at all. Backing this up, Pew finds only 31 percent say they personally belong to a synagogue, temple, or other congregation, including 4 percent of Jews who claim "no religion" at all. Attempting to lead this fragmented population is a bit like herding cats.

The ancient joke about the Jewish Robinson Crusoe tells it best:

> A freighter somewhat off-course in the Pacific spots an SOS smoke signal on a distant island. Stepping ashore, its captain discovers a castaway who has been alone on the island for twenty years.
>
> "What are all these buildings?" the captain asks.
>
> "Synagogues. I built them myself, twenty-seven in all. This one is for Polish Jews, this for Moroccans, this for Yemenites, this for French Jews, this for British, this for Italian, this for..." And he proceeds to identify twenty-six synagogues.
>
> "And that one...?" the captain asks.

The castaway can barely contain his disgust. "That one?" he says, spitting out the words. "That one, I would never go in there."

"Fractious" is a word that barely suggests the divisions among American Jews. If you're looking for Jewish unity or even communality, you might ask a *goy*, or better yet an antisemite.

Merely attempting to assemble this collection of jigsaw-puzzle pieces that will never fit together to make a recognizable picture is simply an unreasonable goal. Which is why top-down administration of American Jewry is all but impossible.

Which is why attempting to organize the defense of American Jewry on a national level is bound to fail. Each synagogue, Jewish center, school, and summer camp is going to make its own choices. At best, Jewish institutions may wish to join together on a geographical basis or ideological basis, probably the single policy with a chance to succeed. That being the case, the wisest course is to encourage all the Jewish institutions in San Diego County or Mississippi to work together despite their differences, or all the Chabad synagogues, which have none. In the face of the threat of violence, this means putting aside theological, social, and political conceits in order to create local security umbrellas.

If this sounds vaguely familiar, such an alignment of necessity in essence defines the national political character of Israel. David Ben-Gurion, Israel's founding prime minister, is sometimes quoted as pointing out the querulous nature of Israel's neighbors: "If we must have enemies, let them be Arabs." What he did not say is that without the Arab threat to throw all the Jews of Israel into the sea, it is likely the Jewish State would never have come to be. The Arabs are divided, but so are we.

When I served in the IDF, my brothers in arms in a particularly well-educated reconnaissance unit—all were college graduates, many with advanced degrees—loved nothing more than to sit around a fire at night exchanging political insults, left against right, religious against secular, in a cacophony of anger, slander, bitterness, and—I am sorry to say—loathing. There, under the stars, I often thought the Arabs would do best by forsaking war and letting the Jews do their work for them. In that sense, maybe the best thing that can happen to unite American Jews as a socio-religious group would be more antisemitism, not less.

At the very least, diverse Jewish institutions, including Jews who are otherwise unaligned, might then come together to create and share policies whose aim is mutual defense against the threat of violence from Jew-haters as diverse as white nationalists, black nationalists, and radical Muslims. Whether this means local sharing of security resources to benefit a broad spectrum of Jewish institutions, renting space at local firing ranges for the instruction of Jews unaccustomed to gun ownership, sponsoring courses in self-defense for children and adults, or otherwise fighting back against threats.

In the 1930s and 1940s, until America's entry into the war against the Axis powers that almost immediately silenced organized antisemitism in the United States—many American Nazis were jailed—the only significant Jewish response came from the least respectable Jews. There was a lot to respond to: At least a hundred antisemitic groups flourished in the US, foremost among them the German American Bund with twenty thousand members and masses of fellow-travelers, followed by such hate groups as the Silver Shirts, the Defenders of the Christian Faith, the Christian Front, and the Knights of the White Camelia. These were not secret organizations: They held public rallies,* marched while carrying Nazi flags, and published news-

---

* At one of these, before a Nazi-packed audience at New York's Madison Square Garden on February 20, 1939, an unemployed Brooklyn plumber named Isadore Greenbaum managed to get on stage in an

papers blaming the Jews for everything from the economy to bad weather. While much of their financial support came from the likes of Henry Ford and cheerleaders for would-be president Charles Lindbergh, the Jewish establishment in the US kept quiet for fear of making things worse.

Less socially acceptable Jews had no such fear. In New York, Meyer Lansky, who would later be denied entrance to Israel because of his criminal ties, organized a relentless year-long assault on the Bund. Here he described to an Israeli journalist how he and his gangster pals, with the help of a large contingent of blue-collar Jews, took care of business at a Bund rally in Yorkville, then a heavily German neighborhood in Manhattan:

> "We got there in the evening and found several hundred people dressed in their brown shirts. The stage was decorated with a swastika and pictures of Hitler. The speaker started ranting. There were only 15 of us, but we went into action. We attacked them in the hall and threw some of them out the windows. There were fist fights all over the

---

attempt to attack Bund leader Fritz Kuhn with his bare hands as the Nazi, in front of a display of giant swastikas, called for a "white, gentile-ruled United States." German-born, Kuhn emigrated in 1926 to the US, where he found work as a chemist with none other than—wait for it—the Ford Motor Company. Greenbaum never actually got to Kuhn, whose Order Division (American for SS) came close to beating him to death before the plumber was rescued by the New York Police Department. The same night, after a magistrate scolded him for interfering with the Nazis' freedom of speech, Greenbaum stated, "When they were attacking the Jews, and so many are being persecuted, I couldn't stand it any longer. I lost my head." Had he been a German Jew, rather than an American, Greenbaum might have lost more than that: Hitler had just finished construction of his sixth concentration camp.

place. Most of the Nazis panicked and ran out. We chased them and beat them up, and some of them were out of action for months. Yes, it was violence. We wanted to teach them a lesson. We wanted to show them that Jews would not always sit back and accept insults."

Business was taken care of similarly in Los Angeles, Minneapolis, Newark, Chicago, and other cities with branches of the Jewish underworld. As quoted by Robert Rockaway in *Tablet*, here is Mickey Cohen, mob boss of Los Angeles, describing a raid on a Bund meeting in California:

> "We went over there and grabbed everything in sight—all their bullshit signs—and smacked the shit out of them, broke them up as best we could…. Nobody could pay me for this work. It was my patriotic duty. There ain't no amount of money to buy them kind of things."

Clearly this *ain't* the grammar of the Jewish establishment, who were nowhere to be seen when the baseball bats came out. As only a few years later, they were equally invisible when Jewish gangsters and Yiddish poets made a last stand against the Wehrmacht in the Warsaw Ghetto. Unused to fighting, unless it was amongst themselves, a dozen Jewish organizations had been unable to come together to deal with the Nazi takeover of Poland. It was no different in the countryside, where criminals and other marginalized Jews took to the forests to harass the Wehrmacht and the SS in guerilla operations that lasted to the end of the war, and in fact may have helped speed its end.

These heroes were not resume-armored administrators hired by the Jewish establishment to defend their brothers and sisters. They were bums in the best sense, with nothing left to lose. They became leaders the same way our Maccabees and Bar-Kochvas did, by stepping forward independently, forsaking defense for offense. It is no accident that in this tradition, the classic battle cry of IDF officers is not "Forward!" but "After me!"

Just as it is understandable that the Conference of Presidents of Major American Jewish Organizations have chosen a graduate of Cambridge University to coordinate and manage a national response to the resurgence of violent antisemitism in our time. One can only wish Michael Masters success and good fortune in this endeavor, though what American Jewry needs at this critical junction is neither management nor coordination.

We need leadership, and that leadership is unlikely to show up in a limousine armed with advanced degrees in criminal law. What leaders will arise in what is likely to be a war for our survival are women and men armed not with diplomas but with desperation, not organizational bureaucrats but individuals who are aware that defense is not enough, and tactical response even less.

What follows are elements of that strategy, which—if it is not yet clear—is not to rest until our enemies are not merely constrained but destroyed.

CHAPTER 14

— ✡ —

Upfront and Digital

Are Jews natural politicians? We must be: Six percent of Congress is Jewish, which is three times our percentage of the US population. But that's only in the House of Representatives. Jews make up 8 percent of the Senate, which is led by a Jew, Chuck Schumer, Democrat of New York. The breakdown by party is more or less as expected: All the Jews in the Senate are Democrats, as they are, with the exception of two Republicans, in the House. Though not all of these are pro-Israel, that number is augmented by members who are. Mostly these represent heavily Evangelical districts.

Yes, there is a new strain, perhaps stain, of anti-Israeli representatives, notably the gang of four Congresswomen self-designated as The Squad: Alexandria Ocasio-Cortez of New York, Ilhan Omar of Minnesota, Ayanna Pressley of Massachusetts, and Rashida Tlaib of Michigan. But with GOP control of the Senate and a Republican president, America's pro-Israel stance is likely to continue. However, a run of Democratic presidents could return us to an earlier iteration of the special relationship between the US and Israel, which is to say much the same but without the bells and whistles. Barack Obama made it no secret that he really disliked Israel's policy decisions—and liked Israeli Prime Minister Bibi Netanyahu even less—but during his administration, military and intelligence ties between the two countries had never been closer. And no matter how far to the left the presidential pendulum swings, it is unlikely the US will move its embassy back to Tel Aviv from Jerusalem, or suddenly decide that the Golan Heights is not part of Israel.

So what's to worry?

Plenty. Congress may be pro-Israel, but it is not necessarily pro-Jewish, the very concept of which is problematic, at best.

What, after all, can pro-Jewish mean in a republic founded on the separation of church and state? The key word here is church, which speaks to a specific, really any specific, group or sect with a capitalized name, whether it be Christian, Mormon, Muslim, Buddhist, or Jew. Once we get past the specific, however, the US is clearly "one nation under God." Which God? Individually we are free to choose. But governmentally not at all. For sure, a bit of specificity has crept in. In many places, so-called Blue Laws kept businesses closed on Sunday, which was considered "the Lord's day" until Jews pointed out it wasn't *their* Lord's day, which claim the courts supported. In that sense at least, the US may be seen as pro-Jewish, but only as much as it is as well pro-Muslim, whose Lord's day is Friday. Certainly, Jewish businesses benefitted by not having to close down on both their own and others' Sabbaths, but if that's being pro-Jewish, then so is the prohibition of quotas for university admissions and membership of country clubs. Both of these, not incidentally, may be more formalistic than realistic. The Ivy League and the local golf club have found their way around what laws exist.

Congress is also not pro-Jewish because there isn't much to be pro-Jewish about. Some European countries—Sweden, Norway, Iceland, Denmark, Slovenia, Switzerland, Lichtenstein, Finland, and two of the three regions of Belgium—prohibit kosher (and halal) slaughter without prior or concurrent stunning. That's not true of the US. The same pertains to bans on infantile circumcision, though a ballot initiative in San Francisco was approved in 2010—the courts later threw it out as, uh, cutting off religious expression. (We'll pause here for readers to supply their own inanely predictable *bris/brit* jokes.) Recent legislative efforts to ban circumcision failed in Iceland and Denmark. Could it happen here, where 75 percent of male babies are circumcised (32 percent in Canada), and the procedure is blessed by the American Academy of Pediatrics as having more health benefits than risks? Though there is no guarantee, probably not.

On the other hand, America's free speech movement, solidly grounded in the Bill of Rights, has had the effect of permitting and even encouraging hate speech. Unless there is a clear call to violence, the Supreme Court has repeatedly ruled that the First Amendment to the Constitution protects hate speech. Calling someone a kike, nigger, mick, wop, or spick is permissible speech, as is marching under Nazi flags and wearing brownshirts while chanting "Jews will not replace us."

In most Western countries, including our neighbor to the north, hate speech relating to race and religion is banned or otherwise restricted. Some countries even ban Holocaust denial, a frequent theme of antisemites. Nevertheless, European antisemitic speech and displays, including violent attacks, not only persist in number and intensity, but have been growing, suggesting one of two scenarios: (a) Antisemitic incidents would be even more frequent were there no laws in place to punish them, or (b) Antisemitic speech and violence would be much the same as it is, despite limiting legislation. One thing is certain, in countries that have vigorous prohibitions against antisemitism, and even those with vigorous enforcement of same, Jew-hatred has not gone away but has found fertile soil in the very political systems that would seem to outlaw it.

Under Jeremy Corbyn, the United Kingdom's Labour Party has been a font of antisemitism for at least a decade. Under the guise of anti-Zionism, Labour accuses Israel of everything from apartheid to the indiscriminate murder of peacefully demonstrating Palestinians. English Jews were once solidly pro-Labour. Today, antisemitism is as much identified with Labour as unionism used to be.

In January 2020, six people, five of whom were Labour Party members, were arrested or interrogated by London's Metropolitan Police for posting messages on social media denying the Holocaust and inciting hatred against Jews. The investigation was based on an internal Labour Party dossier detailing antisemitic activities by twenty-one Labour Party members, which was handed to police in September 2018. The dossier revealed antisemitic social media posts, public comments, written articles, and more made by Labour members. The hateful remarks included, "We shall rid the Jews who are a cancer on us all;" "these Jewish fuckers are the devils;" and a "Zionist extremist MP who hates civilized people" was going to "get a good kicking." Whatever ultimately results, it took the police sixteen months to bring charges, either an indication of how difficult it is to identify users of social media when they don't want to be identified, or how far down the list of crimes hate speech is in the UK.

In the US, it isn't even on the list. Because freedom of speech is guaranteed by the First Amendment, it may not be possible for Congress even to consider legislation forbidding hate speech. Besides which, to take action that is anti-antisemitic is *ipso facto* pro-Jewish. It's true that a combination of presidential and congressional action has provided federal funds for the protection of religious institutions, a policy clearly intended to benefit synagogues and other Jewish institutions—black churches have been shot up and bombed for a hundred years without one federal penny spent to protect them. But Washington has been unable, perhaps unwilling, to meddle in matters of the single major hothouse of antisemitism, the internet.

Ostensibly, this is because internet providers, including such pillars of the US service economy as Facebook, Twitter, Google, and Apple, claim no responsibility for what they carry because they do not originate content. Though radio and television are held accountable for what they broadcast, the internet has escaped this burden, not least on the grounds that monitoring trillions of messages and blogs is all but impossible. Facebook's seventy-five hundred content-monitors are not only playing an endless game of whack-a-mole as the same statements keep appearing under new accounts once the original accounts are shut down, but even defining what is permissible is daunting: In many instances, the same message has been deemed racist by one monitor and permissible by another. Another problem: Hateful blogs are only a small part of what Facebook's monitors are tasked to remove: various forms of pornography, not least kiddie porn, top the list.

The result is that short of intervention by the Supreme Court or a redirection of revenues by internet carriers to remove hate speech, the internet is likely to remain a hothouse for the growth and propagation of antisemitic material and an unassailable means of its delivery.

And given that America's digital giants annually spend millions on lobbying—compared to a pittance by AIPAC, the largest "Jewish" lobbyist, whose interest is solely American support of Israel, not America's Jews—this situation is likely to continue.

As it does in the largest bookstore in the US, if not the world. Feel an urgent need to read *Mein Kampf?* Amazon has multiple editions on sale, including a video subtitled: "The Never-Before-Shown Truth of Hitler's Reich!!" For those of a more scholarly bent, there's *Mein Side of the Story: Key World War 2 Addresses of Adolf Hitler*, either in Kindle edition (free) or paperback. With "Commentary and Illustrations added by MS King," its cover shows a laughing Uncle Adolf amid adoring crowds and a cute photo of the world's most misunderstood guy cuddling a darling little girl. No wonder the book gets five-star reviews from readers who also suggest free copies available on Amazon of works by Holocaust denier David Irving. Here's one from "Matt," who raves (in both senses): "the greatest story NEVER told – The truth about ww2 and the so called holocaust is coming out more and more thanks to the internet. The Germans only wanted peace and were fighting the threat of communism from sweeping throughout Europe. My forever thanks to Hitler and the Germans. I've seen through the lies and propoganda as so many others have."

According to Amazon chief Jeff Bezos in a 1998 speech: "We want to make every book available—the good, the bad, and ugly." When according to ProPublica, a rabbi wrote in to complain about the company selling *The Protocols of the Elders of Zion*, the early-twentieth-century text alleging a Jewish plan for world domination, a former Amazon employee quoted his boss in high *laissez-faire* dudgeon: "Who are we to decide? There's a comments section and people will comment on the fact this is beneath them."

Or not. In fact, Amazon has become the world's largest antisemitic bookstore. According to former employees interviewed for an investigation by ProPublica and *The Atlantic*, "The company's priority—making as much content as possible available to its customers—meant that essentially everything legal was permitted."

Through its Kindle arm, Amazon has become the world's largest publisher of antisemitic literature, a good deal of which can be downloaded for free. Not only that, via its "Customers who read this book also read" section, Amazon has become the world's largest *pusher* of antisemitism. Delighted with *Mein Side of the Story*? Scroll down to where Amazon calls to your attention such *New York Times* non-bestsellers as *Proofs of the New World Order*; *Against Our Better Judgement: The hidden history of how the U.S. was used to create Israel*; *The Program of the Party of Hitler*; *What the World Rejected: Hitler's Peace Offers 1933-1940*; and that timeless classic*, Jewish Privilege*. Space limitations forbid running a complete list of what Amazon has on sale only a click away. As for the how:

> Since its founding more than a decade ago, KDP [Kindle Direct Publishing] has democratized the publishing industry and earned praise for giving authors shut out of traditional channels the chance to reach an audience that would have been previously unimaginable. It has also afforded the same opportunity to white supremacists and neo-Nazis, an investigation by ProPublica and The Atlantic has found. Releases include "Anschluss: The Politics of Vesica Piscis," a polemic that praises the "grossly underappreciated" massacre of 77 people by the Norwegian neo-Nazi Anders Breivik in 2011, and "The White Rabbit Handbook," a manifesto linked to an Illinois-based militia group facing federal hate-crime charges for firebombing a mosque. (Amazon removed the latter last week following questions from ProPublica.) About 200 of the 1,500 books recommended by the

Colchester Collection, an online reading room run by and for white nationalists, were self-published through Amazon. And new KDP acolytes are born every day: Members of fringe groups on 4chan, Discord and Telegram regularly tout the platform's convenience, according to our analysis of thousands of conversations on those message boards. There are "literally zero hoops," one user in 4chan's /pol/ forum told another in 2015. "Just sign up for Kindle Direct Publishing and publish away. It's shocking how simple it is, actually." Even Breivik, at the start of the 1,500-page manifesto that accompanied his terrorist attacks, suggested that his followers use KDP's paperback service, among others, to publicize his message.

Readers in Germany, which bans antisemitic and pro-Nazi publications, can nevertheless download that very thing via Amazon. Clearly, absent similar laws in the US, Jeff Bezos will continue to profit from and promote Jew-hatred in a world that is hungry for it. Is Bezos an antisemite? From all indications, the answer is no. Is he fomenting violence against Jews by providing a marketing platform for those who want us dead? One of Amazon's bestselling nazi authors, one Billy Roper, leads a group which made headlines in 2019 for organizing a protest at a Holocaust-remembrance event, at which they shouted: "Six million more!"

The success of Corbynism in the UK, as well as the rise of antisemitic parties in Hungary, France, Greece, Poland, and Austria, is rarely seen as a threat to American Jews. But it's worth noting that the key to the rise of racist regimes abroad typically begins with hate speech on Amazon and on the internet, a virtual petri dish for the incremental acceptability of hate speech by politicians. Though we are not yet at the tipping point of a Labour Party under Jeremy Corbyn or Hungary's villainous strongman Viktor Orban, we are indeed seeing the development of a slow acceptance of antisemitic speech, in public and on the record. Where previously this kind of thing was limited to the likes of Representative Steve King, Republican of Iowa, recently formally castigated by the House leadership (and amazingly now defeated in a primary), antisemitic mutterings have now transmogrified into a political theme promulgated by the so-called Progressive wing of the Democratic Party.

The members of The Squad see themselves as the vanguard of change for the Democrats. For those familiar with the insidious pronouncements of the UK Labour Party, The Squad's *modi operandi* are eerily familiar, and over time threaten to be very effective: (1) Associate Jews with the alleged sins of Israel; (2) Claim Jews have no god but wealth; (3) Confirm the first and deny you meant anything negative on the second, or that it was taken out of context, or…something you hadn't intended for which you apologize *if* anyone was offended; (4) Increasingly, don't even bother with either evasion.

What is especially galling, if not downright troubling, is the GOP's attempt to paint the entire Democratic Party as antisemitic and antiwhite—it wasn't so long ago that Jew and white were mutually exclusive categories—while at the same supporting a Republican president with a record of antisemitic mumbling in support of white nationalists, antisemitism, or both. Though Donald Trump calls himself "the least antisemitic president ever," who has issued an executive order on combatting antisemitism and points to a Jewish son-in-law and his wife, a convert to Judaism, he has at the same time managed to promote the opposite agenda. On the surface, Trump's us-versus-them political platform may seem to be limited to a them who are brown, but he has let it be known that them also includes "the Jews."

In public, this began with anti-Hillary Clinton electoral advertising in 2016 that included a Star of David enclosing "Most Corrupt Candidate Ever!"; made a stop at telling a (Jewish!) audience how good they are with money; and culminated (so far) in support of nazis in his "There are good people on both sides" statement on the white riot in Charlottesville, Virginia.

That Trump's Republican supporters in Congress keep silent is as scary as the Democratic leadership's not noticing that their own party has been making antisemitic speech legitimate.

In sum, we have elements of both major parties speaking like Jeremy Corbyn, the Democrats via a loud minority and the Republicans via an even more vocal President; the latter shrugging off armed thuggery marching under swastika flags, the former stating unabashedly that Jews are the enemies of economic and social equality. We've seen this movie before in 1930s Germany, where in the struggle for dominance between Communists and Nazis, one matter was not in dispute: It was all the fault of the Jews.

Anyone who thinks there is no oncoming train wreck here is either blind or pretending to be. And anyone who thinks this train is easily stoppable is perhaps worse: dumb. Not only can it be stopped but must be before it derails American democracy in a tragedy whose principal victims will be—guess who—us.

Curiously, the solution to antisemitism as a political tool is using the very same weapon Jews themselves have now and in the past been accused of using to rule the gentile world. No, it's not the poisoning of wells, spreading plague, or kidnapping little Christian children so as to use their blood in baking matzah. It's using our financial acumen to force our will on our hosts.

So let's try that.

If the aim is to suppress and neutralize those using antisemitic tropes—all Jews care about is the benjamins—let's use those benjamins.

If members of Congress can be sent to Washington as a result of electoral campaigns costing $100,000, let's back opposing candidates who don't spout anti-Jewish hatred with $500,000. Let's provide those anti-antisemitic candidates the services of seasoned political operatives in order to displace the goons who have brought antisemitic ravings to the floor of Congress. Certainly the price is right: $2 million would send The Squad back to where they came from—not the third-world countries of Trump's shameful stump speeches, but to their local lairs, there to grumble that the Jews did them in; that, in the political parlance of an earlier century, they was robbed.

Dealing with the on-again, off-again spoutings of a sitting president will be more difficult, but there's enough Jewish money behind him that can be withdrawn and handed over to whoever opposes him. Of course, the Jewish one-percenters who have backed such a president are unlikely to put their mouths anywhere else but where their money is: With rare exceptions, for such people becoming richer in the short term is bound to be a lot more attractive than the long-term viability of the Jews as a people. Enough wealthy Jews were early backers of Hitler so as to ensure defeat of his rivals, the German Communists who would take all that Jewish money. To be fair, both choices then were terrible; today's Progressive Democrats would merely take a lot of Jewish money, mostly in taxes. And let us once again recall the cowardice of the Jewish establishment in the face of Franklin D. Roosevelt's patrician lack of interest in the smoke rising from the chimneys of Auschwitz.

Dealing with unwilling Jews like this and raising money to defenestrate our political enemies will be taken up in a later chapter. Caution: It ain't gonna be pretty.

CHAPTER 15

———— ✡ ————

A War on Hate?

The United States has pretty much been at war against a shifting roster of designated enemies since its founding, also in war. But starting in the last century and continuing seamlessly into this one, America has dedicated itself to war not against enemy states but against concepts, ideas, and things.

How's that been working out?

Starting with the laughable failure that was our War on Alcohol, not so well. Prohibition lasted thirteen years and succeeded mostly in helping crime get organized and making millionaires of rum-runners like Al Capone, who died in prison, and Joseph P. Kennedy, father of our thirty-fifth president, who died in luxury.

This was followed by the tragic failure of our continuing War on Drugs, which has succeeded in filling American prisons with the luckless consumers of illicit products and filling the coffers of international drug cartels with untaxed billions. Both of these "substance wars" cost a fortune in federal, state, and local policing (and the subsequent broadscale corruption resulting from same).

At the same time, for good measure, we had us a nice War on Communism. Distinct from the Cold War, though parallel to it, this one targeted any poor sap a Congressional sub-committee considered "subversive" or un-American or both, which was enough to ruin the lives of thousands in government, education, and the arts, most notably film.

Flushed with failure, the United States then set out on a War on Poverty, whose programs, spanning half a century, have managed from 1975 to today to raise the percentage of Americans living under the poverty line from its original 12 percent to, uh, 12 percent. That's now thirty-eight million Americans, a number greater than the population of Canada. Good job!

Blithely moving on, we are now in the midst of a War on Terror, the success of which may be measured by the spread of Islamist terrorism from Nigeria to the Philippines while leaving in place its nests of origin in the very countries where we dedicated masses of treasure and mountains of corpses to root them out.

Though the War on Terror maintains the dismal distinction of being America's longest foreign war, at base it is just like all the others, which are wars against no enemy that can be shot or taken prisoner, and where no land can be conquered or liberated.

What all these wars, or perhaps "wars," have in common is the feverish delirium that an abstract thought, barely qualifying as an idea, is worth spending trillions on in an inane desire to defeat what is little more than a ghost.

For those hoping for a War on Antisemitism, be careful what you wish for. Hate (arguably love as well) is not only endemic in humans—do animals hate? I don't think so—it is not something anyone can do much about. The expression of antisemitism may be driven underground, as it sometimes is on the internet, but it has proved to be as irrepressible as poverty or the urge for a shot of bourbon or a nice fat joint.

Alas, we Jews are American to the core, as well as creatures of habit, so our much declared War on Antisemitism has concentrated on two approaches: educating the masses that this is just not right (good luck with that) and carpet-bombing the digital topography in which it thrives, just as we did the actual topography of Vietnam and more recently are still busily bombing away that of Afghanistan and Iraq.

Nevertheless, our think-tank warriors have decided, Hey, it worked fine in the Middle East, so why not try making it real hard for various generalized hatreds to thrive on the internet. The outcome so far remains very much in doubt, not least because expunging hatred from a totally anarchic medium may be the most expensive and foolhardy game of whack-a-mole ever.

In "What Twitter Really Means for Islamic State Supporters," a 2015 article posted on the website *War on the Rocks*, author Amarnath Amarasingam interviewed an Islamic State supporter who goes by the pseudonym Abu Ahmad, who has had over ninety Twitter accounts suspended.

> (Abu Ahmad's) online network is important for spreading the new Twitter accounts of individuals coming back from suspension. Watching Abu Ahmad's accounts, for instance, I have been amazed at how quickly he is able to re-acquire his followers. At times, his new accounts are only active for a day or two before getting suspended again, but he manages to get most of his 1,000-plus followers back every time. "I follow people, and they follow me back. We do shout outs," he told me during an interview last month; "we also have secret groups online which don't get

suspended, and we share our new accounts on there."

In a study entitled "The Fractured Terrorism Threat to America," researchers Seamus Hughes and Devorah Margolin of the Program on Extremism at George Washington University summarized the internet's leap-frogging challenges to law enforcement. Their findings reveal that the same tactics used by Islamicists are fully employed by America's white nationalists.

In the mid-2010s, Twitter was the platform of choice for Islamic State supporters. At the Program on Extremism, our colleagues monitored nearly a million tweets by English-language Islamic State supporters. The analysis showed that sympathizers developed active measures for communication and resiliency in the face of account suspensions and takedowns. Sympathizers shared newly created accounts so that others could use them when they were kicked off for violating Twitter's terms of service. "Shoutout" accounts would announce when individuals returned to the platform, allowing them to regain some of their lost followers. For example, we monitored the account of Terrence McNeil, a young man from Ohio who was arrested for reposting an image of home addresses of U.S. military officers with an implicit call for violence toward them. When we first identified the account, he was 7Lonewolfe, but by the time he was arrested, his account was Lonewolfe_18; the increasing number in his handle reflects a constant game of whack-a-mole against his account, which was disabled at least 11 times.

Following the aggressive removal of accounts from Twitter and an even more aggressive (monitoring of) social media by law enforcement agencies, many English-language jihadist supporters transitioned to platforms offering more privacy and operational security. A major example is Telegram, an online instant messaging application that offers some encrypted communications tools.... The downside of this transition to platforms like Telegram is that homegrown terrorists are less likely to appear on law enforcement's radar as they move to more niche sites. It is not simply jihadists who are learning this lesson. Indeed, we have also seen a recent shift to Telegram by white nationalists.

Under federal pressure in 2017, Microsoft, Twitter, and Google partnered with other international organizations to found the Global Internet Forum to Counter Terrorism. The idea was to control the spread of terrorist propaganda online. As described above, the likely outcome is that extremist content will continue to be pushed off monitorable platforms but find their way to what the FBI calls "going dark," which is to say moving to the fringes of the internet where the FBI has limited ability to track it. Internet companies say they are tracking and removing evil content where they can. Facebook alone says it has seventy-five hundred content monitors detailed to keeping it off. It hasn't worked. When it comes to statements like "Remove the j's from earth," how can anyone but the poster and the clued-in reader know that "j" does not stand for jungles, jaguars, or jellybeans?

Does this sound a lot like throwing money at a problem and hoping it sticks? Alas, the problem is not the use of the internet by white nationalists, jihadists, and just plain unclassifiable Jew-haters, it's the *existence* of those white nationalists, jihadists, and Jew-haters.

Short of extra-judicial killing, either by the government or vigilantes, neither of which is at the moment an operable solution, it might be far better to disrupt the lives of those at the top of the hatred apex. Oddly, this may be accomplished within the law. And maybe by stretching it.

CHAPTER 16

—— ✡ ——

Trial by Jewry

The US is chock full of lawyers, more per capita than any other nation. In fact, Jews represent 6.6 percent of American lawyers, over three times the percentage of Jews in the general population. Assuming a few might be reading this, the sharper minds among you might already have figured where this is heading.

Case in point, and I do mean case: *Bollea v. Gawker.*

A professional wrestler better known by his professional name of Hulk Hogan, Terry Gene Bollea in 2013 sued Gawker, a website, for invading his privacy and intentional infliction of emotional distress by showing a sex tape involving Bollea and another professional wrestler's wife. If you're thinking nobody can make this stuff up, stay tuned. Enter billionaire Peter Thiel, founder of PayPal, who had earlier been outed as gay by none other than…Gawker. Hearing about the case, Thiel subsidized Bollea's legal costs with $10 million of his own money. Three years later, a jury awarded the wrestler $140 million in damages. Though later significantly reduced, the award was enough to close down Gawker, which was unable to pay. According to Thiel, his motivation was "less about revenge and more about specific deterrence."

Aha.

In using the law's power to admonish, punish, prohibit, and deter, Thiel's employment of massive financial firepower to break the back of his enemy may be seen as high-handed, but no one can say it did not work.

Can such a strategy defeat antisemitism? It can't. Defeating an ism just doesn't work.

But it can (a) stop actual flesh and blood antisemites who promote lies about Jews and incite violence against us, and (b) in so doing, deter others from the same. Locking antisemites up in years of legal battles, to say nothing of the cost of defense, might very well put them out of business. With some luck, a judge may even temporarily forbid further antisemitic statements by the defendant until the case has been adjudicated, which could take years.

Is this unfair? From the point of view of the targeted antisemites and the free speech absolutists who would oppose it on principle, yes. From another point of view, this is like the question of whether Israel uses "excessive" force to suppress Palestinian violence. Should the IDF be limited to fighting rock-throwers by throwing rocks back at them? If so, logic demands Jews should counter antisemitism on the internet by publishing blogs to educate the world in general and antisemites in particular about how nice we are.

The hell with that: We Jews must use every weapon at our disposal. A War on Antisemitism will never be successful, but a War on Antisemites stands a good chance of cleaning their clocks.

Alas, lawyers rarely work for free. Getting individual lawyers to monitor the wonderful world of antisemites—on the internet, on the streets, on campus, and in business—while administering and coordinating an effort to suppress them is not going to be easy. We'd need an organization dedicated to doing just that.

The Lawfare Project is already doing it, and has been since its founding in 2010 by a charismatic Canadian-born lawyer named Brooke Goldstein. Its mission is to provide "*pro bono* legal services to protect the civil and human rights of the Jewish people worldwide." Considering that it is under-staffed, under-funded, and, even among lawyers, under-known, its success is as gratifying as it is improbable. When its own staff is unable to handle a specific case, either because it requires more time or greater expertise, the Lawfare Project reaches out to some 350 lawyers in sixteen jurisdictions worldwide to do the work *pro bono*. So far it has brought seventy-four actions and initiatives.

Its list of cases won is as impressive as it is a staggering reminder of how widespread antisemitism is and how diverse its expression. Some examples:

Who knew that Kuwait Airways unlawfully discriminates against Israeli passport holders by refusing to fly them on any of their routes? Answer: Israelis trying to catch a convenient flight out of New York's John F. Kennedy Airport or London's Heathrow. After alerting the US Department of Transportation, the Lawfare Project forced Kuwait Air to comply with federal (and foreign) law or lose its lease at JFK. Though it would be nice to hear that Kuwait Air chose the former, instead it canceled its popular JFK–London route, with losses in the millions. If this sounds like tolerable losses to the flag carrier of a desert kingdom that could burn dollars instead of jet fuel, the Lawfare Project has also sued Kuwait Air in Switzerland and the United Kingdom, which shut down all its intra-European flights. Eventually Kuwait Air may not be able to fly anywhere other than within the Arab world unless it agrees to board Israeli passport holders. Next stop: Saudi Arabian Airlines. The lesson here goes far beyond the boarding lounge: No matter how well financed, no company should be able to discriminate against Israel, and by extension against Jews. According to Goldstein, "We will not stop until we facilitate Kuwait Airways coming into compliance (with international law) or not flying at all."

When Saudi Arabia refused to grant a visa to Israeli chess players to prevent them from competing there in an international tournament sponsored by the International Chess Federation (FIDE), the Lawfare Project worked to have the tournament moved to Russia, which doesn't discriminate against Jews, at least not in chess.

The Lawfare Project is especially active when universities actively discriminate or passively refuse to protect the rights of Jewish students and faculty.

In 2019, in partnership with the 160-year-old California law firm of Winston and Strawn, the Lawfare Project reached a settlement in which San Francisco State University agreed to take measures to protect Jews on what may be the most viciously antisemitic campus outside of Teheran.

In New York, the Lawfare Project and co-counsel Corey Stark filed suit against Kingsborough College of the City University for unlawful employment discrimination against a Jewish faculty member.

On the criminal side, the Lawfare Project enlisted a team of three attorneys to provide *pro bono* assistance to a college student who was assaulted by a supporter of Justice for Palestine, which might as well be called Injustice for Israel.

These examples make it clear that American higher education is in the grip of an antisemitic fervor that can be controlled only by vigorous pursuit of a square deal for its victims as a deterrent to future acts of hate.

But the Lawfare Project has so far limited itself to what I'll call proper use of the law to protect Jewish rights. About as far as the group stretches outside these limitations is sending warning letters to companies bowing to the Boycott, Divestment, and Sanctions (BDS) movement, which seeks to choke Israel economically through international boycotts. The Lawfare Project calls this "counseling (corporations) on the legal implications (and penalties) of discriminatory commercial conduct." And it has been working.

What the Lawfare Project does not do is what Peter Thiel did by backing Hulk Hogan in a lawsuit whose aim, however unstated, must certainly have been putting Gawker Media out of business.

To this end, I can't help thinking of the parallel to America's Cipher Bureau, which, beginning in World War I, cracked the codes of enemy nations and, often enough, allies. Until 1929, that is, when incoming secretary of state Henry Stimson killed the Cipher Bureau on the grounds that "Gentlemen do not read each other's mail."

Eventually gentlemen did, to the extent that the National Security Agency, of which the Cipher Bureau was a precursor, now seems to be reading everyone's mail. It is America's largest intelligence agency. And with the creation in 1947 of the CIA from its own wartime precursor, the Office of Strategic Services, gentlemen would not only read each other's mail but send each other letters full of misdirection—and sometimes plastic explosives.

If nations can use dirty tricks, why should America's Jews snub the practice, in this case using the law à la Peter Thiel?

I'll leave it to the lawyers to make sure they are not later accused of torturous interference with commerce—is promoting nazi violence commerce?—but I'm all but certain there is a case to be made for suing antisemites of all stripes so they may have their day in court to defend against civil, and perhaps criminal, prosecution, and another day in court, and another, and another, until they, like Gawker, are either sick and tired of threatening Jews or, God bless America, broke.

CHAPTER 17

Campus Disruptus

I n 2014, two professors at Trinity College in Hartford, Connecticut published a little noticed *National Demographic Survey of American Jewish College Students*. According to Ariela Keysar and Barry A. Kosmin, 55 percent "of Jewish college students report experiencing anti-Semitism on campus in the past year." Admittedly, the survey is theoretically out of date, but considering how reports of antisemitic incidents in the general population have risen in the interim, the situation on campus is likely not to have improved. According to the latest information from the US Census Bureau, in 2017, 18.4 million students were enrolled in American colleges and universities. If we consider that Jewish students make up some 5 percent of all college students (Jews are 2 percent of the general population, but much more likely to attend university), that comes to about one million students who experienced some form of antisemitism. According to Keysar and Kosmin, this was "mainly from an individual student." Assuming this is unlikely to be the same student, the statistic suggests perhaps a million separate antisemitic students. And that is among the "educated" cohort of American youth. Try to imagine the level of antisemitism among those whose last year of education is tenth grade.

Nevertheless, there's worse hiding in the survey, which reports that "more than 66 percent of the students are always 'open' about their Jewish identity on campus." Which means, *ipso facto*, that 34 percent of Jewish students are not always open about being Jews. Clearly, if all of these suddenly began wearing tee-shirts with Jewish stars printed across the front, we'd see nearly two million incidents of antisemitism.

This suggests that Jewish college students are unlikely to avoid Jew-hatred on campus. Of course, the nature of that antisemitism must be taken into account. If it's murder, that's one thing. If it's getting involved in the losing end of a political argument, which on college campuses means a lot of sound and fury signifying misplaced adolescent angst, that's another. But clearly, we're not talking here of murder. We're talking about social snubs, snide insinuations, and perhaps drunken revelations of what is normally left unspoken. We're talking about Arab and pro-Arab leftist students shouting down a pro-Israel speaker. We're talking about a radical left-wing professor refusing to call on an Israeli or identifiably Jewish student because she is a "Judeo-Nazi" or "a Zionist liar."

As uncomfortable as this may be, and though unlike mass murder such improprieties are likely to be *under*-reported, this isn't *Kristallnacht* by a long shot. American campuses are and have always been hothouses of unrestrained political and social emotion, both on the part of students, who are for the first time feeling their oats away from parental restraints, and on the part of the professoriate, which is largely tenured and, thus free of potential penalty, may fearlessly promote the idea that the moon is made of green cheese and that the evil Israelis are eating it all up.

There is of course the unsettling prospect that in twenty years the radical students we love to hate will turn out to be a new generation of teachers at all levels, including university professors, to say nothing of government officials and even American presidents. But who is to say what the world will look like in twenty years? Perhaps it will follow the course of the ancient Yiddish story of the Jewish finance minister who falls out of favor with the king and is sentenced to hang the next morning.

> The Jewish minister asks the king, "Your highness, will you agree not to hang me if in a year I can teach your dog to speak?"
>
> "If you can teach my dog to speak in a year," the king says, "I will spare your life."
>
> Afterward, the minister's good friend takes him aside. "Are you crazy? How are you going to teach the king's dog to speak?"
>
> "In a year," the Jewish minister answers, "I could be dead, the dog could be dead, or the king could be dead."

Very nice, you say, but what about the present? "My son is being subjected to antisemitism at (fill in your favorite problematic) university! Someone called him a Zionazi!"

Tsk, tsk. It's a tough world out there, isn't it? My advice: If junior can't handle it on his own, he can call a local office of the Anti-Defamation League (ADL), where someone is likely to tell him free speech is free speech, but a bloody nose is assault. In fact, the ADL devotes an entire section of its website to what to do about campus antisemitism. Boiled down, unless a law has been broken, the answer is not much. With President Trump's recent executive order adding antisemitism to the legal prohibition of discrimination based on race, sex, or age, this may change. But executive orders change as well, with one president's Mede being another's Persian.

Where incidents of antisemitism are so egregious as to be legally actionable, counselors at the ADL and/or *pro bono* attorneys at the Lawfare Project should be able to offer necessary assistance.

For students just learning that Jew-hatred exists, the best idea might be to join their school's Hillel, where your child's experience is unlikely to be its leaders' first antisemitic rodeo. At last count, there are five hundred and fifty branches of Hillel on US and Canadian campuses and another forty-four abroad. At bottom, these are places where young Jews can find a sympathetic ear and, conceivably, assistance. If your children are studying at a school that does not have a Hillel chapter, this may say a good deal about the way you raised them. Perhaps worse than the shock of discovering antisemitism may be discovering that others consider them to be Jews. Mazel tov! Welcome to the club. A lot of people don't like Jews. That's not the problem. The problem is a lot of people want to kill Jews. Admittedly fewer. For the moment.

CHAPTER 18

─────────── ✡ ───────────

Mosaic Fragments on the Lobby Floor

W hen we hear about the "Jewish lobby," critics almost always mean AIPAC, the American Israel Public Affairs Committee. Recently the noise began again with Rep. Ilhan Omar's claim that Jews are undermining democracy by supporting AIPAC. This was followed by an article in *The New York Times* headlined, "Has AIPAC—founded more than 50 years ago to 'strengthen, protect and promote the US-Israel relationship'—become too powerful?" (*Nota bene:* Substitute "The United States Chamber of Commerce" for "AIPAC" in that headline and ask yourself if such an article would ever appear in *The New York Times*.) To cement the idea that AIPAC is a "Jewish" thing, the online version featured a guy in *tefillin*. This cleverly turns the canard that antizionism is not antisemitism on its head: According to *The New York Times*, to support Israel as the only democracy in the Middle East is just a Jewish thing. This will come as news to those among AIPAC's supporters who are Evangelical Christians or just plain Americans who see Israel as a dependable American ally. In any case, AIPAC is laser-focused not on satisfying the Hannuka wish list of the guy with the *tefillin* but, mostly, the armaments budget of the Israel Defense Forces.

Considering the noise, one would think AIPAC is the gorilla of Washington lobbyists. It's more like one of those tiny monkeys people keep as pets but can still bite. AIPAC doesn't make anyone's list of largest lobbyists, though it may be one of the most effective.

With a 2018 lobbying budget of $3.5 million, the price of a dozen filet mignon dinners at Washington's Bourbon Steak (I exaggerate: average dinners cost $160) or an evening at The Old Ebbitt Grill, the oldest restaurant in the District of Columbia and one of the nation's highest grossing, two of a dozen places where the capital's *nomenklatura* regularly eat and drink on someone else's tab, AIPAC's spend is barely a rounding error compared to the big boys. Who are they? Have a look: The US Chamber of Commerce ($94.8 million in 2018), the National Association of Realtors ($72.8 million), Israel-critic George Soros's Open Society Policy Center ($31.5 million in 2018), Pharmaceutical Research and Manufacturers of America ($28 million), American Hospital Association ($24 million), Native American casinos ($22 million), Google mother-company Alphabet ($21.7 million), and Facebook ($12 million).

Compared to AIPAC, lobbies for a couple of dozen minor *Jewish* organizations—including museums, Holocaust memorials, and religious groups—in total spent only just over $1 million in 2018. This is chump change.

Which is a problem.

American Jewry numbers some seven million (or six, depending on who's counting and by what standard—I prefer to use Jean-Paul Sartre's: If others think you're a Jew, you're a Jew). By whatever standard, we're certainly more numerous than the 5.5 million members claimed by the National Rifle Association, which in the past two years spent $9.6 million on lobbying. This is not to be confused with the nearly $55 million in campaign contributions the gun group spent in the 2016 presidential elections (fully $31 million went to the Trump campaign). Purely on lobbying, the NRA spends five times the amount as all the Jewish groups combined, and there are more Jews in the US than NRA members. Clearly there is something wrong with this picture.

Of course, on the basis of two Jews, three opinions, getting American Jewry united on all the relevant issues is not going to be easy. It is also not necessary.

Arranging to get Chabad in the same room as the Rabbinical Council of America, both Orthodox but with little love lost between them, is hard enough without attempting to include a group like Keshet, which is "for LGBTQ equality in Jewish life." With no Vatican to decide on what Judaism is and isn't, we're hopelessly but gloriously fissured: When it comes to Jewish life, the word *mosaic* is in both senses appropriate.

But just as Apple and Microsoft—arguably in the same business—each fields its own lobbyists to forward its own specific interests, so too can Jewish organizations, each with its own agenda. Because at least some of those agendas may be the same.

For instance, considering that President Trump's executive order on protecting Jewish institutions from violence may not be extended by his successor, can we not unite on working for Congress to make it law? How about pushing for legislation offering funds for religious organizations to *actively* protect themselves from attack, perhaps calling them "community organizations" to leapfrog the Constitution's church/state provision? With European "progressives" echoing the prejudices of Nazi

Germany, if not the Roman Empire, in calling for bans on ritual slaughter and male circumcision, complaints about which are beginning to be heard in the US, why not press for laws that make them legal or, in a word we all know and some of us love, kosher?

Like many synagogues, my own in Southampton, New York was compelled to pay a fortune in legal fees, in our case $1.2 million, just to keep its doors open in the face of a local ruling that considered a synagogue to be in violation of residential zoning. Apparently, the massive Roman Catholic church and rectory several doors down the street was not a problem. In another instance, a synagogue in a neighboring village was required to spend heavily on lawyers to contest a ban on setting up an *eruv*, in this case a perimeter of fine nylon fishing line strung from electricity poles that defines the perimeter within which on the Sabbath religious Jews may carry personal articles and push baby carriages. In dozens of localities, the same cases have already been adjudicated, invariably in favor of permitting zoning for synagogues and setting up an *eruv*. In both these instances of what is apparently passive antisemitism gone ballistic, federal law would help by superseding local ordinances in much the same way the Voting Rights Act of 1965 overrode decades of Jim Crow. After all, the Constitution stipulates freedom *of* religion, not *from*.

Jewish lobbying need not be limited to articles of faith.

Who gets admitted to colleges and universities and on what grounds ultimately affects all Jews. So too does the public display of Nazi symbols, which some claim is freedom of speech but which are truly little more than graphic threats of mortal violence against Jews, regardless of whether said Jews are religious, atheist, agnostic, or merely nominal. The first may be tricky, but the second might well not be struck down by the Supreme Court: Can anyone claim that the swastika means anything other than "Let's kill the damned kikes?"

Currently, internet providers are exempt from the restrictions on hate speech that govern television and radio, though both came about as a result of federal innovation and investment of everyone's tax dollars. But the internet is as much the product of government as the licensing of broadcast channels: the Pentagon's ARPANET provided the World Wide Web its initial technology. Should not America's digital giants be held responsible for the instigation of racial murder on their distribution channels? Though Microsoft, Apple, and Google overwhelmingly outspend Jewish lobbies, online antisemitism is for sure one thing that most Jews will agree should be controlled, if not outright forbidden.

On a deeper level, perhaps Congress, which Mark Twain called "America's only native criminal class," might stop brawling long enough to define racism and racist. For years now, the Supreme Court has ruled these terms to be protected speech, not subject to charges of defamation. In *Forte v. Jones*, the Supremes in 2000 found "statements indicating that Plaintiff is racist are clearly expressions of opinion that cannot be proven as verifiably true or false." In 2010, this was confirmed in *Edelman v. Croonquist,* in which the court ruled "racist has no factually-verifiable meaning." Very well then, let us ask our distinguished solons to pass legislation giving these words a factually verifiable meaning, so that Jew-haters can be made to pay for calling Israel racist and Jews racists. That way, Jews can call real racists racist.

Not least when they display the swastika or other regalia associated with Nazism. What other meaning do these symbols have other than "Kill the Jews?" This is not a free speech issue. It is quite the opposite. It is an incitement, whether in words or symbols, to murder. Such incitement is illegal in other countries—why is it countenanced here?

Defining racism—whether hanging a noose outside the dorm room of a black student or painting a swastika on a synagogue—is the kind of thing Jews should be lobbying Congress to make nationally illegal. This hardly exhausts the possibilities of substantial lobbying efforts on behalf of America's Jews, perhaps in coordination with other minorities. As to the question of who pays for all this, we'll get there.

CHAPTER 19

◇

The Enemy of My Enemy Is My Friend

Concerned that I was on my way to having a great future behind me, in 1967 I quit a perfectly good job as the youngest reporter at *Newsday*, then an ambitious but stodgy Long Island newspaper that insisted its journalists write only using the news-English that was already a collection of clichés in the 1930s. Worse, it was difficult to get an article in the paper that went much further than local politics or really bad house fires. In those days, magazine writing was changing all that in its use of language, not simply to describe significant events, but to create them. So I quit to freelance. My first assignment was from *The Village Voice*, the mother of America's underground weeklies, which was actually going to pay me for traveling to Mississippi to cover a murder trial.

I couldn't drive down fast enough.

The year before, three young civil rights workers lost their lives at the hands of the usual suspects for that time and place, white segregationists of little distinction other than a shared propensity for violence. On the other hand, their victims were unique, young men willing to risk their lives for the cause of racial justice in the south: James Chaney, a black Mississippian, and New Yorkers Andrew Goodman and Michael Schwerner, who were white. But not just white.

They were Jews, heroes really, naive as all get out.

Not that I mentioned this in the article I turned in, which was immediately rejected by the *Voice's* founding editor, Dan Wolf. I had violated a key tenet of left-wing journalism: Say nothing good about (a) the South, or (b) Dwight D. Eisenhower, the Republican president who in 1957 federalized the Arkansas National Guard to escort Afro-American children into a determinedly all-white school in Little Rock. In offering background to the revolutionary verdict of guilty brought by a Southern jury in a race-based murder, I called it the beginning of a new era below the Mason-Dixon Line, noting as well the imperishable fact that a Republican president had fired the first shot in killing off Jim Crow.

"You can't say that about Eisenhower," Wolf told me. "This is *The Village Voice.*"

A man of his times, Wolf was simply an old-school left-winger who refused to be confused by the truth that race relations in America were complicated. And still are.

Which is why, as I went on to other things, I remained fascinated by the conundrum of Jewish-Black relations, both at the national and local levels. I had long been aware of black antisemitism, which then was merely anti-whiteism with a twist. In 1960, I had graduated from Thomas Jefferson High School, which drew its very mixed but hardly integrated student body of fifty-five hundred from across two Brooklyn neighborhoods,

East New York and Brownsville, that then had the highest murder rate in the city—a record which persists to this day. Once a predominately Jewish area, by the time I ran for student-body president, it was about a two-thirds mix of "Negroes" and newly migrated Puerto Ricans. Directed by word-of-mouth to the non-white majority, my unofficial electoral slogan—it got me elected, then suspended—was *Vote for the White Guy.*

The joke was, there were other whites running for office, but I was the only one known to the non-white students as "the white guy," not least because I was one of the few Jews who sat with non-whites in the cafeteria.*

In my own naivete, I saw myself as a bridge between the two communities, so much so that when I got to *Newsday,* a white suburban newspaper where everyone but me had a mortgage, covering civil rights fell in my lap by default: No one else on the staff had ever even met "coloreds," much less socialized with them (or, as adolescents, fought with them). When in the summer of 1967, Harlem exploded in rioting, I was dispatched

---

* This was probably a result of a peculiar social dysfunctionality of my mixed-race neighborhood, and probably that of others around the country. In elementary school, it had been common for me to visit non-white friends in their homes, and them in mine. It would have been strange not to: My next-door neighbors were black. But with the onset of puberty, I found myself unwelcome in the apartments of black friends, especially those with sisters. The last thing any black family wanted was inter-racial romance. In those days it was dangerous to be seen in public with a person of the opposite sex outside your own racial category. One way or the other, it meant trouble. So, the only time I could socialize with the kids I had grown up with was at school. Much later, as a foreign correspondent working in Africa, I was sometimes asked if I wasn't afraid of being surrounded by armed and often angry blacks. Often I was—the Congo was hardly my Brooklyn high school. Invariably my answer would be: "Do you know where I grew up?"

like a western movie half-breed scout to bring back word on the hostiles.

The next day, with the rioting continuing, my editors presented me with a shiny white motorcycle helmet. Noting that it was not the kind of thing one wears to a riot, I explained, "It seems to be missing a bullseye painted on it."

My editors at *Newsday* didn't have a clue. But maybe I didn't either. Like Rodney King, victim of a severe beating in 1992 by Los Angeles police, I couldn't understand why we all couldn't just get along. After all, I was one of the few whites I knew who had grown up with black friends.

Some years later, on a fine Yom Kippur afternoon, taking a break from synagogue on a visit to my parents, now moved to the somewhat less distressed nearby neighborhood of Crown Heights, I was walking along its main thoroughfare, Eastern Parkway, when I became aware that a car with four young black guys was trailing me.

"Hey, Kestin, what you doing all suited up around here?"

May I be forgiven for saying so, but that could have been the best Yom Kippur of my life, even many decades of High Holy Days later. We decamped to the nearby apartment of one of my former inmates at Thomas Jefferson, where we smoked enough grass to inspire a bit of an epiphany. My hosts talked with great specificity about all the white girls they hadn't been able to date (I believe date was not the word) and I talked about my parallel frustrations on the other side of the racial divide. Even high, I realized one couldn't be a bridge between Jews and blacks when the shores I wished to connect kept growing apart.

In 1990, I returned to the US after twenty years in Israel, only to find black-Jewish relations to be even worse than black-white. Never mind Michael Schwerner and Andrew Goodman, never mind that Jews had been among the founders and supporters in 1909 of the NAACP. Economic and social conditions had improved marginally for Afro-Americans, but astoundingly for Jews. Jews with professional degrees were now the norm; despite many who had climbed into the middle class, American blacks by comparison had been left in the dust. The camps were segregated by wealth, education, and social standing. When my father arrived in America in 1939, Jews were barely considered white. Fifty years later, the bleach of financial success had done its work.

For reasons too complicated to describe here, this has left us with a legacy of black resentment and anger facing off against Jewish indifference and—now—fear. But considering that both peoples are the descendants of slaves and that both are all but defined by a history of suffering, how is it not possible for us to come together against a common enemy? Considering the growth of nazism in America, is it not clear that if we do not hang together, we will hang separately? Surely Jews and blacks, along with a growing American minority of Latinos and other slices of the demographic pie, ought to be able to pool our strengths for the common good.

At this point, the cynics among us may ask: Yeah, yeah—but to what end?

First and foremost, to pool our resources. Jewish legal and political skills fit very well with the massive electoral power of that *other* other. When it comes to white nationalists, Jews and blacks have a good deal to fear, and good reason to work together. The same goes for the Latino community and America's similarly broad array of Asians. What unifies us, or should, is that we have all been targeted and will remain targeted by white nationalist hate and violence. The same legislation that Jews ought to be demanding to protect our synagogues and cultural centers ought to be fought for by other minorities. I don't recall any push by black leaders in 2015 for federal aid to protect black churches after nazi Dylann Roof slaughtered nine African-Americans at a church in Charleston, South Carolina; not in 2019 either, when over a ten-day period, three black churches were burned to the ground in central Louisiana.

In 1963, when Ku Klux Klan members planted a bomb in the 16th Street Baptist Church in Birmingham, Alabama that killed four African-American girls, Martin Luther King Jr. called it "one of the most vicious and tragic crimes ever perpetrated against humanity." What followed? More black church bombings, fires, and shootings: from 1995 to 1997, there were 827 attacks on black churches. Oh yes, President Bill Clinton set up a commission to look into this, and Congress created the Church Arson Prevention Act of 1996, which did nothing to prevent church arson but merely stiffened the existing penalty from ten to twenty years in jail for "defacing or destroying any religious real property because of race, color, or ethnic characteristics."

While it's true that a National Fire Protection report found that only (only!) 16 percent of such fires were arson, that is still a lot of arson, and that does not include the kind of attacks on black churches that prefigured the shootings at Pittsburgh and Poway. For those of us who roll our eyes at the racial posturing of Black Lives Matter, consider for a moment the fact that while all such attacks are equal, some seem to be more equal than others.

There is something to be said for the kind of democracy of self-interest that has created the federal and state lobbying industry, which pits money against money in what can seem like a dining table battle for more chicken. Maybe as Jews we ought to give this more thought. It could be that a system that pits one minority against all others satisfies none but the indifferent majority.

Does it not make sense that we should share the effort and expense of working together for a shared agenda?

Is it not clear that Asian-Americans now face the same college-entry quotas confronting Jews decades earlier, and which, despite Ivy League denials, continue to this day? As I write this, Asian-Americans who have never been to Wuhan, China face abuse on our streets for their alleged responsibility in the spread to America of coronavirus. Would it be so awful for the Cohens to sit down with the Wongs in order to put the screws to institutionalized racism in our universities and in public, and for good measure, invite in the Jeffersons and the Velazquezes, many of whom are no longer sure affirmative action is all that they'd hoped. And is the treatment of would-be immigrants from Central America, to say nothing of their children, something that should not be a Jewish issue? When Jews complain that the lessons of the Holocaust are being forgotten, do those lessons apply only to Jews?

We must also look at finding political common ground with Evangelical Americans. We're talking about what Pew's 2020 Religious Landscape Study found to be one in four Americans. That's a lot of potential allies. Certainly with regard to Israel, Evangelicals far exceed the electoral clout of Jews (2 percent of the population); just one Evangelical group, Christians United for Israel, claims seven million members, about the same as America's Jewish population. A report by the American Jewish Committee found that the number of Jews who agree that "caring about Israel is a very important part of my being a Jew" declined from 70 percent in 2018 to 62 percent in 2019. A recent Pew Research Center survey found that 42 percent of US Jews say Trump "favors the Israelis too much," while just 15 percent of US evangelicals agreed with that statement. If that sounds like Evangelicals on a per capita basis are more committed than Jews to the Jewish State, this appears to be true. According to *Travel Weekly*, 61 percent of visitors to Israel, 4.5 million in 2019, identified as Christian. This means twice as many *goyim* come to Israel as tourists than Jews. During the recent coronavirus pandemic, the International Fellowship of Christians and Jews set up a $5 million fund to provide Israeli hospitals with respiratory equipment and aid to elderly Israelis in need. Despite the organization's name, its membership is overwhelmingly gentile.

But there is more than Israel to bind the two groups. Like Jews, Evangelicals send their children to religious or religiously affiliated schools, which means both groups have an interest in federal and state aid to private education. Can it be that Yeshiva of Flatbush and Birmingham Christian Academy have a lot in common? Only in America.

Which brings us to Muslim-Americans, about 1 percent of the population. Normally considered an adversary demographic, it turns out that apart from presumed disagreement on what goes on in the Middle East, mosque-goers and *shul*-goers have mutual concerns about what goes on in the Middle West. That's where a good deal of kosher and halal meat is slaughtered. Attempts by humane-slaughter groups, notably People for the Ethical Treatment of Animals (PETA), to outlaw kosher and halal slaughter are not going away, and in Europe are gaining ground. As to another accusation of unkind cuts, it happens that both Muslims and Jews favor male circumcision, the former by tradition and the latter by religious law. The right to do so is as well under fire in Europe, and there have been similar mutterings in the US.

American Jews seem to have gone out of our way to ignore opportunities to build bridges with other minorities.

In 1986, the Supreme Court ruled the Constitution did not require the military to accommodate an Orthodox Jewish captain's challenge to a regulation prohibiting the wearing of a skull cap while in uniform. In 2017, the Army all on its own decided to allow Muslim soldiers to wear hijabs and to permit Sikhs turbans and religiously mandated beards, along with *kippas* for Jews. In the intervening years, did Jews spearhead a demand for Congressional hearings so they could state their case with

Muslims and Sikhs? Why the hell not? Did all of us minorities have to wait thirty-eight years to see a military dress code that takes into consideration that America is no longer a melting pot but a salad bowl?

Of course, antisemitism is not only coming at us from the white right. It is also a feature of the black and—more recently—Hispanic left. Which is bizarre when we consider how many people are black *and* Jewish or Latino *and* Jewish. Though the number of the first group is uncertain—a Pew Forum 2014 survey found non-white Jews to be 2 percent of the Jewish 2 percent—many of us know of Jews who are black, or part black, which in the US is the same. (Note: We're not talking of sects like the Black Hebrew Israelites, who claim to be the real Jews, not us). And we're not talking of black Jews in history, like Willie "The Lion" Smith (whose father was a Jew, and who could lay down a nice line in Yiddish) or converts like singers Sammy Davis Jr. and Jackie Wilson.

We're talking about recent examples, among them Lenny Kravitz, Drake, Daveed Diggs, Craig David, Sophie Okenado, Maya Rudolf, Lisa Bonet, Tracee Ellis Ross, Lauren London, Amar'e Stoudemire, Rashida Jones, Shyne, Tiffany Haddish, Lani Guinier, Walter Mosley, Nell Carter, Carolivia Herron, Jamaica Kincaid, James McBride, Carol Conaway, Lewis R. Gordon, Naomi Zack, Lawrence Thomas, Darrin Bell, Ephraim Isaac, Yaphet Kotto and Lacey Schwartz. Richard Pryor? Nope. But his daughter Rain is.

This list could go on a while, but the real list should include thousands of names you never heard of, not least a dozen rabbis of many persuasions, including Capers Funnye, a cousin of Michele Obama and the first African-American member of the Chicago Board of Rabbis.

On the Hispanic side, intermarriage has produced a similar number of Latin Jews, to say nothing of Jewish immigrants from

Mexico and Cuba, and in the last decade or so from Central and South America. That list? We don't have the space, but as it happens Joaquin Phoenix, Geraldo Rivera, and David Blaine are Jews by the strictest Orthodox definition: Jewish moms.

A 2011 survey by the United Jewish Appeal of the eight counties making up the New York City metropolitan area found that "the large number of biracial, Hispanic, and other 'non-white' Jewish households—particularly pronounced among younger households—should serve as a reality check for those who are accustomed to thinking of all Jews as 'white.'" What's a large number? A quarter million people living in eighty-seven thousand households.

That's a lot of "others" to have on our side, and a nice wedge into the radical left theology that Jews are some sort of monolithic assembly of benjaminites whose sole aim in life is suppression of other minorities. It turns out many of the latter are also the former. Really, what are the members of Congress known as The Squad to make of Alma Hernandez, who at twenty-five is the youngest member of the Arizona legislature? Mexican-American, Jewish-American, Progressive, *and* pro-Israel, should she ever be elected to Congress she would be one-woman proof that them is also us.

Well aside from actual dual identities, we've shown in so many instances that Jews have enough in common with other minorities that pulling together may redound to our mutual benefit. Yet there is more to be gained than political power in state legislatures and in Congress.

Imagine what would happen if the next time nazis march on an American street, the counter demonstration is composed not only of Jewish-Americans but Afro-Americans, Latino-Americans, Asian-Americans, and perhaps even Muslim-Americans, who are as much the targets of American nazis as we are. Should push come to more than shove, as it almost certainly will, I'd want the Association of Hyphenated Americans on my side, wouldn't you? And yes, that does work out to AHA!

CHAPTER 20

Check Please

Outside of those of us who have more money than we can spend, anyone who has built a house, bought a car, or ordered a bottle of wine is faced with choosing between desire and affordability. A bathroom in the basement is convenient, but at forty thousand dollars could be pushing it. We may really want to go from zero to sixty in 2.8 seconds, but that's worth another sixty grand. As to a fifty-dollar bottle versus the nearly as good for twenty-three, maybe that's best left for special occasions, like some other time.

American Jewry is faced with similar choices. Ideally, every synagogue in the US and Canada should be a bulletproof, bomb-proof nazi-resilient fortress. We should have whole platoons of armed guards to protect our schools, community centers, and day camps. We should dedicate millions to teaching our children to hit back and our adults to fire a gun. We should be spending at least as much as the NRA on lobbying government to preserve our rights. We should move Jewish money to support candidates all over the country who oppose the antisemites who have recently cropped up in Congress. We ought to spend on outreach to other minorities so we can work together to get what we all deserve. While we're at it, we should sue the hell out of white nationalists, black radicals, and Islamists when they attempt to harass and silence us, and while we're at that, harass and silence them right back when they use the internet to foment and crystallize hatred of Jews, even if that means going head-to-head with such cash-swollen giants as Facebook and Google.

In short, we should raise billions to do everything in our power to make sure no one disrespects, threatens, or does violence to us or to our children.

Can we?

Anyone who has ever attempted to raise money comes up against one or more stock objections: (a) I give too much as it is; (2) I don't give to your cause because I don't believe in it; (3) Worth considering—let me think about it.

Persistence helps, of course. That's where the bother factor comes in: people give just to make you go away. The shame ploy often works too and people don't want their name not to appear in the yearbook or engraved on the wall of benefactors. It's also possible to convince people to unsheathe their checkbooks based on the merits of your cause, but an appeal to pride works better. As a Jewish film producer in a book of mine trumpeted: "I gave a wing to Cedars of Lebanon…. You can't die of cancer in LA without reading the name EZ Shelupsky."

But speaking generally, the easiest way for people to open their wallets is the threat of pain. Antisemitism? That's an abstract. Combatting antisemites is better, but still a bit distant. Jews who live in massive apartments on Park Avenue may be shocked at the attacks on synagogues in middle-class spots like Poway in Southern California and Squirrel Hill in Pittsburgh, but they've got doormen downstairs, elevator operators, a foolproof security system in the penthouse apartment itself, and they travel only by chauffeur-driven limo and private jet. Their children attend schools no terrorist can get into—not without paying eighty thou a year—and the synagogues they support but rarely visit are ringed by security.

A good fundraiser might be able to find a chink in all this armor, but mostly the very wealthy are insulated from societal threats (street crime is something that happens many floors below, in other neighborhoods) and even protected from health hazards (for the rich, no waiting for a medical appointment next month or cooling their heels in an emergency room for half a day), and if treatment is not covered by health insurance, so what?

It may be that the only fundraiser who is certain to walk out with a donation is one with a gun to the donor's head. Don't laugh. This kind of thing has been working in our country since before it was a country. It may not be taught in the schools, but a good deal of the money to bankroll the American revolution came from those who had been made an offer they couldn't refuse.

Let's hope it doesn't come to that today. But what we can be sure it comes to remains that pesky matter of hard choices regarding how to spend our limited funds on crushing antisemites before they crush us.

Straightaway, it's no good looking at what American Jews currently spend on Jewish institutions and charities. We're not about to close some synagogues to pay for the protection of others, or to shutter hospitals and orphanages or even day camps. The idea that to protect American Jewish lives we must destroy American Jewish culture is as ludicrously impractical as it is self-destructive. Burning down a country in order to save it did not turn out well in Vietnam; nor will it work in Jewish

America. The simple conclusion is since we can't tighten our belts, we must loosen our purse strings.

And since, as we have said, the Jews have no pope, such decisions are going to be made by large organizations considering the greater good—for instance, the cost of lobbyists, whose efforts if successful would affect Jews nationally—or by individuals and communities more tightly focused on problems closer to hand, like securing the entrance to the community center.

Paradoxically, though popeless, we do have a *curia* in the form of those self-anointed cardinals who make up the leadership and administrative bureaucracy we know as the Jewish establishment. As we've seen, depending on this perennially out of touch "leadership" is historically a joke verging on tragedy. America's Jewish organizations are all about individual self-aggrandizement, that photo op with whomever is resident in the White House, a trip abroad to represent American Jewry at the Vatican or, second best, in Jerusalem. As with anything worth doing right, we must be prepared to do it ourselves.

It's on us.

Whatever "it" is will mean a serious financial burden at every level of American Jewish life. Rather than attempt to break down the costs of everything we'd love to do to protect us into the future, it might be interesting to try to understand what we can afford.

(1) According to the US Census Bureau, annual spending for public education from pre-kindergarten through high school averages just over $12,000 per pupil. That totals some $700 billion, all of it raised from taxes, most of it on real estate via local school districts. Some districts, like New York City, just about double that. Question: If we were forced to raise this sum voluntarily, would we be able to do it?

(2) The net (after grants) annual cost of private colleges is about $20,000 per student, half that at public colleges.

Assuming a family saves for four years of college, which is a voluntary cost but for most families a socio-economic necessity, this means through high school graduation putting aside $6,700 a year for private schools and $3,350 for public schools. That's for the basics. Rounding the numbers to make them easier to visualize, and taking into consideration the looming possibility of graduate school, a family would have to put aside $10,000 a year for private colleges per child and $5,000 a year for public.

(3) There are about seven million Jews in America. If we skim two million "marginals" off the top—never mind that the Jews Hitler targeted included more than those who self-identified as Jews—that leaves five million, or on the back of an envelope, about two million families.

(4) Now we're getting somewhere. If each of these two million families were to kick in $1,000 a year for a total of $2 billion, presumably that would pay for everything on our self-preservation wish list, and then some. But as we've seen, getting people to commit to voluntary taxation is not easy. So let's be more modest in our goal. Rather than $1,000 a year, let's knock the yearly voluntary tax to one hundred. At $200 million, that's still quite a working treasury, but collecting it might still be an obstacle. What about ten dollars a year?

Bingo.

We have arrived at $20 million. And from so low an average contribution that it may be possible; some not giving at all, some giving a good deal more. After all, ten bucks is two cups of Starbucks' Caramel Macchiato (Grande) plus keep-the-change. How this might be raised is an open question, but remember please that most will be put together locally to meet local needs. Will it be enough?

That depends on how we prioritize our needs. Each of us will have differing requirements, but for me, the ladder of requisites starts with investing in our children so that they grow up confident in their Jewish identity and their ability to defend it physically. As with any quality investment, that's not something we'll profit from tomorrow, but a new generation of strong Jews, both within and without, is probably the best investment we can make. Whether this turns out to be Jewish day schools or meaningful daily study after secular school will be up to each of us. If this very basic requirement does not come into being, we will have a situation wherein our children's generation will be attacked for being something they can't comprehend. Am I talking religion here? No, I'm talking religion or culture or history or whatever combination each parent decides is best. Whether Orthodox, Conservative, Reform, or secular, a Jewish education is the most basic requirement for our survival in an increasingly hostile world. And with that, let us please have our kids taught how to disable an attacker. If they can master the backhand return on the tennis court, they can learn *krav maga*.

Next on the list, and one of the most cost-effective, is learning to become familiar with firearms. I've been warned repeatedly that this is just not a Jewish thing—please see Chapter 21—and I'm aware that Jews have long been in the forefront of the anti-gun movement. But even committed pacifists must learn to defend themselves. To permit, much less encourage a situation in which our enemy is armed to the teeth and we are ducking behind desks is about as childishly delusional as the political posturing of those Israelis willing to accept peace at any price. If the price of peace is death, who in their right mind would wish it?

On a more pragmatic level, the expense of hiring armed guards to protect our religious and social institutions is so high, and so cost-ineffective, we have simply got to do it ourselves. Aside from the cost of guns, which cost may be applied to protecting one's home and family, the only real expense is for large signs outside our synagogues, schools, and community centers:

PROTECTED BY
THE WRONG JEWS

As to spending on hardening our institutions with bullet-proof glass and iron gates and window grates, on alarms and flashing lights, and on other props of passive defense that can be easily overcome or neutralized, I believe this amounts to the kind of security theater in which we are forced to participate every time we board a plane. Just as any intelligent terrorist can get through airport security with a bomb or a knife while uniformed clerks are busily confiscating cologne and nail clippers, so too can a high-school drop-out nazi dispatch an armed guard with one bullet to the head. As we've seen, a rifleman sheltering behind a car across the street can wipe out a dozen people as they exit the synagogue.

The only real defense against antisemitic violence is to identify and root out those who want us dead.

This calls for both national and local efforts. Sleuthing existing databases of internet Jew-haters, we must identify these by legal name and current address and then go after them via law enforcement, if that is relevant, via civil law if that works, and via guerilla lawfare by tying them up in the courts and breaking them financially. Once terrorists have been identified, alternative offensive activities may be considered: where lawful suppression of our enemies proves ineffective, innovative measures may be required. While vigilantism is no panacea, it is worth considering what assassinating Hitler might have accomplished before he became absolute ruler of Germany.

No matter which of these iterations we choose, the cost will be high to employ hundreds of computing experts just to locate the real people hiding behind internet identities. Some legal work may be *pro bono*, but at a certain point, attorneys will have to be paid.

At the same time, American Jews should be dedicating our wealth and political expertise to prevent the election of antisemitic federal and state legislators. To block the election of a single Congressional candidate is likely to cost half a million dollars; a senator, twenty times that. This is simply acting prophylactically: Once antisemitic tropes are seen to draw organized Jewish opposition, they are likely to occur less often. To do this right, we must add to AIPAC, whose activities are focused only on America-Israel relations, the establishment of a political action committee dedicated only to the empowerment of the American Jewish community. Call it the Jewish American Political Action Committee, call it JAPAC, or call it something else. Under any name we must will it into existence.

Only then will we have the clout to lobby government at all levels to make sure Jewish rights are not only protected but expanded. Considering that the National Rifle Association spent $9.6 million over 2018 and 2019 to sway Congress and state legislatures to condone a state of affairs that is anathema to half the electorate, American Jewry must do at least as much to neutralize the influence of those antisemites who, by their own admission in poll after poll, make up a quarter of the electorate. If not half.

When it comes to defeating Jew-haters, offense is truly the best defense. But any general will tell you that offense is a lot more expensive. Adding a $20 million tax to the cost of being Jews in America, even at ten dollars annually per family, is going to be a tax that may only be collectible once things get a lot worse. Let's hope American Jews can leave aside standing together and instead act together before that worse happens. As with any disease, the cost of prevention is a lot more effective than the cost of treatment—and a lot less fatal.

CHAPTER 21

A Jewish Dentist

In 1987, I took a break from the daily stress of living in a Jewish state to take over *Forbes Magazine*'s London bureau, which covered Europe, Africa, and the Middle East. After living rather primitively, if not hand-to-mouth, on a farm in Israel for almost two decades, London was Cinderellaville: In the twinkling of an eye, I had become a somebody, armed with a great salary and an expense account whose limits I was all but invited to test by Malcolm Forbes himself, who insisted I join a club and get my suits bespoke, as he did, at Huntsman. As the wife of a prince of the foreign press corps, Leigh was invited to the Queen's Garden Party (and bought a hat so as to properly curtsy while saying "Hi" to Princess Di and "Mum" to the Queen Mother). My kids were at school with the sons and daughters of members of Parliament, celebrated actors, and well-known novelists. As a journalist, there wasn't a world leader I couldn't arrange to chat with or chairman of a major corporation who did not wish to impress me, or rather through me *Forbes'* readership, among the world's best-heeled investors.

Having spent years as proper Israelis in an unheated farm-house whose roof-top solar panels were sufficient on the sunniest day to provide hot water for only two showers for a family of six, with a washing machine that often worked, and a line out back to dry our few items of clothing when it did, we found ourselves suddenly living in an elegant carpeted flat in Holland Park, whose panoramic view looked out over a good part of London and conveniently overlooked its class structure. Our neighbors in Israel were farmers, mechanics, and others who worked with their hands, if not their backs; in Holland Park, they consisted of the idle rich, the working rich, high-ranking diplomats— three embassies were on our block alone—the chairmen of major banks, and, most impressive for a movie-lover like me, Sean Connery.

Perhaps most revolutionary was that I no longer carried a gun.

As a journalist in Israel, I was always finding myself in what American film westerns used to call hostile territory, and of course, during what averaged out to be a couple of months of reserve duty in the IDF, I slept and ate with my M-16 close to hand and a Colt Combat Commander 9mm pistol on my hip. Of course, London was not free of crime, but little if any found its way to Holland Park. On the contrary: Were I to carry a gun here, I would be the criminal. Which probably explains my confusion one Sunday afternoon when I bumped into my first real nazi.

My son Ross was eight at the time. We were just returning home from finishing off a couple of slices of pizza. And there he was, as real a nazi as any I could have imagined. Dressed head to foot like some diabolical reincarnation of the SS, he may have been stylistically over the top—a single death's head insignia is just too many—but clearly not shy about advertising his politics.

About thirty, heavily built, and wearing both a thick leather jacket and motorcycle boots, he was also a walking threat: a one-man invasion of a genteel neighborhood that may not itself have been home to many Jews, but also certainly was not the kind of place that welcomed nazis in full regalia. If there were antisemites in Holland Park, they were of the "*upper-clahss*" English sort, defined by Isaiah Berlin as "Someone who hates Jews more than is absolutely necessary."

Perhaps because I had grown up in a Brooklyn neighborhood where fistfights were likely to break out at any time, I sized up my nazi and quickly concluded I could work around that thick leather jacket and take him with a swift kick in the nuts followed by a full-on punch to the face. Though I hadn't been in a street fight in decades, I was just over forty, in good shape, and fully capable of tearing every disgusting Nazi insignia off his clothes; and if that didn't work, tear off his clothes and leave him naked on Holland Park Avenue. Then I came to my senses.

Here I was holding the hand of an eight-year-old boy making a mess of his face with a melting ice cream bar. If I beat the stuffing out of the man, would my son see his father arrested for assault? If things went wrong, would little Ross himself be in danger? Though I was pretty sure I would make short work of my nazi, what if it went the other way? There is never certainty in a street fight: What if the bastard was carrying a knife?

In an instant, I made the decision. Someone else would have to do what circumstances would not permit. A couple of decades later, again walking with Ross, this time on the Rue du Rhône in Geneva, I had a second chance.

Ross was now pushing thirty to my sixty. Instead of a face full of ice cream, my son—the middle child of five and the most ambitious—had turned into a very successful adult managing billions of dollars in client money. He had just treated his old man to a very expensive lunch, not pizza. But we had come upon the same nazi.

Well, not precisely. This one was a skinhead, no peaked cap with death's head insignia, but plenty of swastikas and, though it was summer, he was wearing a leather jacket, the back of which we found ourselves following down the very crowded shopping street. We could hardly miss that jacket: it was one big swastika. Beyond that, I could see little of who this Nazi was. He was certainly younger than me—I was getting to an age where everyone seemed to be—but appeared to be my size. We had been following him for a block, well past the building where my son worked.

"Go to your office," I told Ross quietly in Hebrew. "You've got work to do."

"Not going to happen, dad."

"Nothing's going to happen."

"Then it's a nice day for a stroll, isn't it?"

Both of us knew the two of us would have no trouble hospitalizing our nazi. Ross alone could have handled him. Years before, I had stopped sparring with the kid. He was now a man, strong from hours in the gym, and quick. The last time we had tussled, I had reflexively defended myself with a very dirty move from the Brooklyn streets. He had looked at me then, shocked I was not playing fair, and probably shocked as well that his old man was, in fact, too old to do anything else.

"I can handle this," I said.

"Of course," Ross said. "But it's better together."

As before, I considered. Ross had spent years creating a business built on two factors: his inherent talent in managing client funds and the fact that he was in Geneva, where Swiss banking laws kept those funds secret and secure. If we went ahead with this, the chances were good we would be arrested for assault. Switzerland does not countenance street crime. Nazi or no nazi, there would be a felony conviction. Jail was not a certainty, but for sure Ross's hard-won residency permit would be revoked.

"Just listen to your father and go back to your office."

He laughed.

I stopped walking. Ross stopped as well. "Not worth it," I said as we watched the swastika lose itself in the crowd. "Probably just a nut job."

What our second nazi was, and possibly even the first, was a harbinger of things to come. I did not know that then. Today things are different. Both Ross and I would know that instinctively. We would have to act. Getting rid of nazis is like getting rid of roaches. Once a few are allowed in, they multiply. Pretty soon your home is not your own. It's not a free speech issue. It's a matter of survival.

Albert Camus, now not much read, said it best: "Real generosity towards the future lies in giving all to the present."

Which is pretty much what this book is about. We must be aware that the seventy or so years since the liberation of the death camps are not, as we so blithely thought, the beginning of a new age, but have been instead a hiatus, a vacation from the history that has plagued and defined the Jews for thousands of years. The antisemitic violence we thought was dead has returned, and by all indications with a vengeance.

The question is therefore not only what we should do, but when.

Putting off the inevitable may mean permitting another inevitable to establish itself, as it did in Germany in the 1930s. Had German Jews done more than stand together, we might not have had an Auschwitz. Assaulting the guilty on a street in Berlin might have prevented what was perhaps the greatest ever assault on the innocent in recorded history. Stopping our own nazis, black, white, or Muslim, defeating those who want us dead, is not a question for the future. It is a matter for now.

The overriding question is, and sadly I must return to it, are we capable of putting aside the centuries of passivity bred into our bones, as well as today's refusal to get our hands dirty because we have become a generation of lawyers, doctors, professors, accountants, and dentists?

For a hint that we may be more than we appear to be, I offer this excerpt from a citation awarding the Congressional Medal of Honor posthumously to an officer in the United States Army in World War II.

> Captain Ben L. Salomon was serving at Saipan, in the Marianas Islands on July 7, 1944, as the Surgeon for the 2d Battalion, 105th Infantry Regiment, 27th Infantry Division. The Regiment's 1st and 2d Battalions were attacked by an overwhelming force estimated between 3,000 and 5,000 Japanese soldiers. It was one of the largest attacks attempted in the Pacific Theater during World War II. Although both units fought furiously, the enemy soon penetrated the Battalions' combined perimeter and inflicted overwhelming casualties. In the first minutes of the attack, approximately 30 wounded soldiers walked, crawled, or were carried into Captain Salomon's aid station, and the small tent soon filled with wounded men. As the perimeter began to be overrun, it became increasingly difficult for Captain Salomon to work on the wounded. He then saw a Japanese soldier bayoneting one of the wounded soldiers lying near the tent. Firing from a squatting position, Captain Salomon quickly killed the enemy soldier. Then, as he turned his attention back to the wounded, two more Japanese soldiers appeared in the front entrance of the tent. As these enemy

soldiers were killed, four more crawled under the tent walls. Rushing them, Captain Salomon kicked the knife out of the hand of one, shot another, and bayoneted a third. Captain Salomon butted the fourth enemy soldier in the stomach and a wounded comrade then shot and killed the enemy soldier. Realizing the gravity of the situation, Captain Salomon ordered the wounded to make their way as best they could back to the regimental aid station, while he attempted to hold off the enemy until they were clear. Captain Salomon then grabbed a rifle from one of the wounded and rushed out of the tent. After four men were killed while manning a machine gun, Captain Salomon took control of it. When his body was later found, 98 dead enemy soldiers were piled in front of his position.

The citation ends: "Captain Salomon's extraordinary heroism and devotion to duty are in keeping with the highest traditions of military service and reflect great credit upon himself, his unit, and the United States Army."

Maybe it should have included "on Jewish dentists," for that is what Ben Salomon was. He could just as well have been a Jewish accountant, lawyer, or businessman. One thing is certain: Ben Salomon was not bred for heroism. Descended as he was from two millennia of Hebrews whose method of survival was taking it on the chin, Captain Salomon was not a professional soldier but a draftee, placed by circumstance at the peculiar intersection of character and opportunity.

American Jews are coming to this intersection now, if not already arrived. Clearly, few of us are Ben Salomons. For one thing, Captain Salomon was not faced with a choice: Either he fought or died. As it turned out, he did both. Ben L. Salomon was obviously a unique individual, with great reserves of strength, anger, and resilience. Facing overwhelming odds, he absolutely refused to give in.

It may also be true that Captain Salomon was of another generation of American Jews, tougher than the present crop, less refined, more willing to take on a challenge that can only be called existential. If that is so, we are in a great deal of trouble, because our enemies—like the suicidal waves who eventually overcame Ben Salomon on Saipan—are not like us. Like the Nazis of the previous century, today's Jew-haters are the resentment-driven losers of a society that values and honors what American Jews have accomplished, and thus they are compelled, even to the point of sacrificing their own lives, to destroy ours.

And the lives of our children. If only for them, each of us must find what we can do to contribute to the defense of our people by defying and defeating those who want us dead. Because if we don't, from all indications these pathetic lower-case nazis will be triumphant.

For those who insist it can't happen here, the bad news is that it is already happening. But the good news is we can stop them now before they become too strong, before their illness infects the general population as it did in Germany, before it is, like it or not, too late.

Let us then resolve to stand up to the challenge, so that afterward each of us may be privileged to say, "When they picked on me, they picked on The Wrong Jew."

Remsenburg, New York
April 2020